THE ACROPOLIS
THE ACROPOLIS MUSEUM

The marquis de Nointel, ambassador of the French king Louis XIV at Constantinople, and his escort at the foot of the Lykabettus hill, with Athens and the Acropolis in the background. J. Carrey, oil on canvas, 1674. Permanent loan from the Musée des Beaux-Arts of Chartres to the Museum of the City of Athens Vouros-Eutaxios Foundation.

KATERINA SERVI

THE ACROPOLIS
THE ACROPOLIS MUSEUM

EKDOTIKE ATHENON SA

General publication editor: Christiana G. Christopoulou
Editor: Maria Koursi
Translation: Despina Christodoulou
Art direction: Spyros Karachristos
Cover: Dimitris Tsalkanis
Photography: Ilias Georgouleas, Manolis Petrakis, Ekdotike Athenon Archive
Accounts: Evangelia Kotsiri
Secretariat: Maria I. Tsoutsi
Orders: Giorgos Kaberis
DTP: E. Varvakis & Co

ISBN: 978-960-213-452-8
Copyright © April 2011, Ekdotike Athenon SA
13 Ippokratous Street, Athens, 106 79
Tel.: +3020-3608911, Fax: +3020-3608914
email: info@ekdotikeathenon.gr
www.ekdotikeathenon.gr
Printed and bound in Greece

CONTENTS

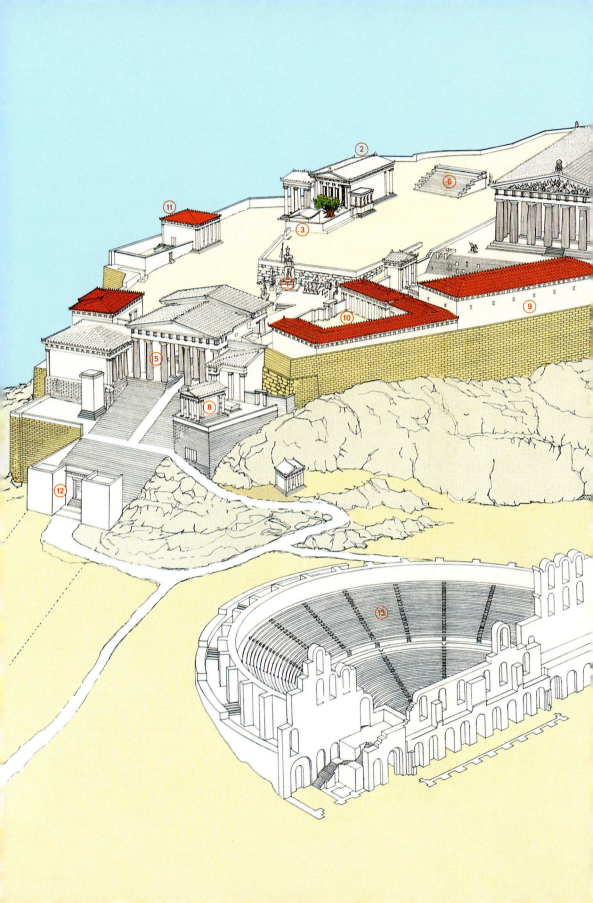

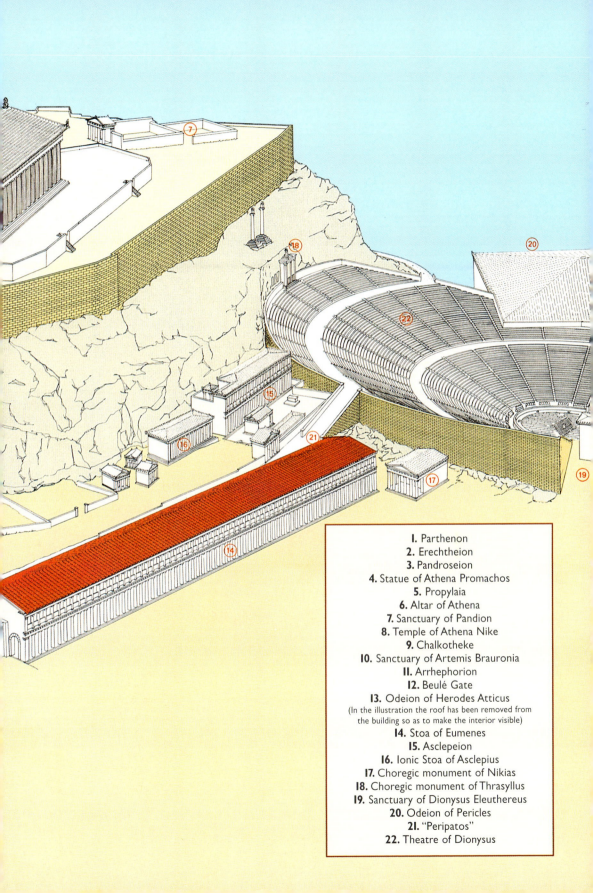

1. Parthenon
2. Erechtheion
3. Pandroseion
4. Statue of Athena Promachos
5. Propylaia
6. Altar of Athena
7. Sanctuary of Pandion
8. Temple of Athena Nike
9. Chalkotheke
10. Sanctuary of Artemis Brauronia
11. Arrhephorion
12. Beulé Gate
13. Odeion of Herodes Atticus
(In the illustration the roof has been removed from the building so as to make the interior visible)
14. Stoa of Eumenes
15. Asclepeion
16. Ionic Stoa of Asclepius
17. Choregic monument of Nikias
18. Choregic monument of Thrasyllus
19. Sanctuary of Dionysus Eleuthereus
20. Odeion of Pericles
21. "Peripatos"
22. Theatre of Dionysus

A GLANCE AT HISTORY

Prehistoric and Geometric eras

A small, sun-drenched plain with a precipitous rock at its centre, a broad platform at its peak and valuable springs with drinking waters at its foot. The people of the prehistoric era could not have ignored such an advantageous site. And indeed, excavations at the top and the slopes of the Acropolis have revealed traces of settlement dating from the late Neolithic period (*ca* 3500-3200 BC). This habitation continued over the following periods, the Early Bronze Age (3200/3000-2200/2000 BC) and the Middle Bronze Age (2200/2000-1600 BC).

In the second millennium BC the population of Attica was reinforced. A new tribe, the Ionians, arrived from the north and merged with the indigenous population, which tradition holds were the Pelasgians. From around the middle of the same millennium a brilliant prehistoric civilisation started to flourish on mainland Greece, the Mycenaean civilisation which took its name from its most important centre, the town of Mycenae. During the Mycenaean period (1600-1100 BC) the inhabitants of the Acropolis lived in groups on the slopes and at the peak of the rock. They worshipped their ancient goddess Athena here, on the top of the Acropolis hill, where the palace of the local king also stood.

There are few remains of the architecture of the geometric period, but this excellently preserved clay model of a temple from the Argive Heraion enables us to form an image of the earliest Greek temples. Athens, National Archaeological Museum.

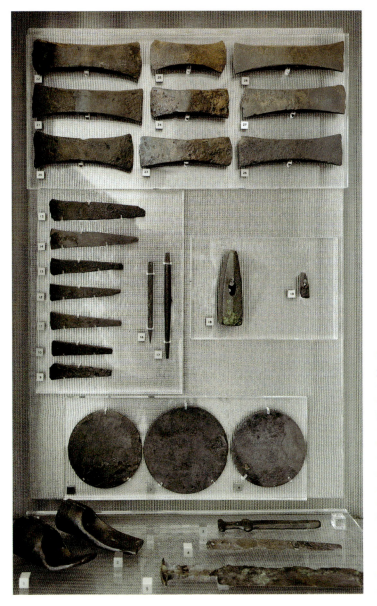

In the legendary Mycenaean period, the fortified Acropolis rock thronged with life. The finds from this distant period include vases, figurines and other objects, as well as the exceptionally interesting Coppersmith's Treasure. This is comprised of a group of bronze weapons and tools, the possessions perhaps of a Mycenaean coppersmith, which were found hidden in a wall of the Mycenaean Acropolis and dating to 1190-1130 BC. Athens, Acropolis Museum, Level 1, Archaic Gallery, case 4.

During this period, the 13th century BC, the flat area at the top of the Acropolis was fortified with giant walls, similar to those of other Mycenaean towns, which also protected the entrance at a deep crevice in the rock leading to a water spring, the Mycenaean well. In later times the walls of the Athens Acropolis and the acropolises of other Mycenaean towns started to be called 'Cyclopean' because the people were so impressed by their size that they imagined they had been built by beings with supernatural powers, the giant Cyclopes. The fortification of the

Bronze disk with cut-out sheet from the earliest geometric temple of Athena on the Acropolis. The terrifying figure represented here is the Gorgon or Medusa, one of the three mythical sisters with the bodies of monsters and snakes instead of hair. The hero Perseus cut off the head of the deadly Gorgon and gave it to Athena, who attached it to her shield.
7th century BC. Athens, Acropolis Museum, Level I, Archaic Gallery, NAM 13050.

Mycenaean Acropolis was reinforced with the addition of a second wall at the foot of the hill, the so-called 'Pelargic' or 'Pelasgic' wall. It was later called the Enneapylon, as it had nine gates. One reason for its construction was to protect the springs on the north and south sides of the rock.

The 'synoecism' is also dated to the 13th century BC, the process, that is, whereby the small communities that up till then had comprised Attica were amalgamated into one city, with Athens as the common political centre. The Athenians of the classical period believed that this process had been carried out by the mythical king Theseus.

This was followed by the so-called 'descent of the Dorians' (late 12th century BC) and the collapse of the Mycenaean world. The Dorians, as tradition holds, attempted to invade Attica, although without success. In the later Geometric period (1100-700 BC), so-called because of the use of geometric shapes on pottery decoration, the city grew into an important commercial and artistic centre. Our knowledge of the Acropolis during this distant period is limited. Research, however, has shown that already from the 8th century BC a small temple was built on the site of the Mycenaean palace, described by Homer as the 'pion naos' (wealthy temple) and the 'pykinos domos Erechtheos' (sturdy house of Erechtheus). It was dedicated to Athena Polias, protector of the city.

Archaic Era

Over the next centuries the foundations were set for the city's great political and cultural flourishing. By the 7th century the institution of the king had declined and the political system of Athens had evolved into an aristocracy. This situation was changed somewhat at the end of the century by Dracon, who granted political rights to a broad section of the Athenians. He even codified the law, instituting penalties for violators that tradition holds were particularly harsh, hence the term 'draconian'. This was followed by a period of social upheaval, as a result of the debts endured by the peasants. Solon, however, was to appear on the political scene in the early 6th century BC. His political and legislative reforms were of vast significance, easing the situation and paving the way for one of the greatest achievements of the Greek spirit: Athenian democracy.

Athenian history in the mid-6th century BC is associated with the ingenious and exceptionally ambitious aristocrat Peisistratus. Although he usurped power as a tyrant, Peisistratus governed as a moderate and contributed greatly to the city's economic and cultural development. In addition to his love of letters – the Homeric epics were written down for the first time in his day – Peisistratus particularly encouraged the arts, and he is attributed with the reorganisation of the Panathenaia, the ancient annual festival in honour of the goddess Athena. This reorgani-

The goddess Athena, the patron of Athens, was often called Promachos ('foremost fighter') because she helped people in battle and, more generally, during their difficult moments. Bronze votive figurine of Athena Promachos from the Acropolis, 475 BC. Athens, Acropolis Museum, Level I, Archaic Gallery, NAM X6447.

sation took place in 566 BC and every four years since then the Panathenaic celebrations were particularly grand, and hence known as the Great Panathenaia. Scholars believe that Pesistratus' initiative was connected with the great building activity that is observed on the Acropolis during this specific historical period. It was at this time that the first large temple to the goddess, the Hekatompedon, was constructed, on the spot where one hundred years later the Parthenon would be erected. Next to the grand new building with the colourfully-painted pediments were some smaller sacred buildings ('houses') and numerous votives, dedications by the faithful to their beloved goddess. Those making dedications included both aristocrats as well as artisans, men and women, who, as the inscriptions from the surviving pedestals tell us, offered them as gifts either as the *aparchi* (the first income from their work), or as a *dekati* (one-tenth of their income).

Peisistratus' sons Hippias and Hipparchus succeeded him after his death in 527 BC. The Peisistratid regime was shaken in 514 BC when Hipparchus was assassinated by Harmodius and Aristogeiton, the Tyrannicides. Several years later, in 510 BC, the tyranny came to an end.

The end of the century was marked by the reforms of another great legislator, Kleisthenes (508/7 BC), whose radical reforms laid the foun-

◀ *The goddess Athena, with the aegis that terminates in snakes covering her left wrist, attacks the Giant Enceladus, known through tradition; only the lower part of his leg has survived, which cannot be seen in the photograph. This grand piece comes from the east pediment of the goddess's 'old temple' on the Acropolis, which was decorated with a scene from the Gigantomachy, the battle waged by the gods of Olympus against the rebellious sons of Gaia, the Giants. 525-500 BC. Athens, Acropolis Museum, Level I, Archaic Gallery.*

Archaic Athenian hoplitodromos – the road race in which athletes ran in armour. The man wears an Attic crown and wields a spear and round shield with a satyr as emblem, the mythical creature with an animal-like face and horse's tail. Of interest is the inscription with the name Glaucytes and, underneath, the half-erased Megacles, the name of a member of a large Athenian aristocratic family. This name may have been replaced when Megacles was exiled from Athens. Painted clay plaque from the Acropolis, 510-500 BC. Athens, Acropolis Museum, Level I, Archaic Gallery, case 25.

dations for Athenian democracy. It was perhaps during this period that another temple, the 'old temple' of Athena, was built to the north of the Hekatompedon.

The 5th century was ushered in with wars between the Greeks and Persians. The first phase of fierce battles ended with the victory of the Athenian troops, thanks to the genius of the general Miltiades at Marathon in 490 BC. Immediately following this, the Athenians began the construction of a large marble temple on the Acropolis in order to thank their patron goddess. This temple was never completed. In 480 BC the Persians, who had invaded Greece for the second time, were able to reach as far as Attica and set fire to Athens and the Acropolis. A little later the Athenians, urged on by the far-sighted general Themistokles, abandoned their houses and fled to the neighbouring island of Salamis. Soon, however, the momentum of the enemy expired. At the battle of Salamis the Athenian war fleet, a creation of Themistokles, crushed the Persians. And a little later, in 479 BC, after the Greek victory at the battle of the Plataea, the Persians retreated definitively. As soon as the Athenians returned to their city, they reverently buried whatever remained of the sacred buildings and the votives on the Acropolis in the natural cavities of the rock. They incorporated some pieces of the dismembered buildings into the north wall of the Acropolis, where they have remained until today.

Classical Era

The victorious wars over the Persians marked the end of one era and the beginning of another, the most glorious in the history of Athens and the Acropolis.

In 478/7 BC the Athenian general Aristeides put together the Delian League or the first Athenian League, an alliance of island and coastal cities in the Aegean that sought to continue the struggle against the Persians. Its seat was the holy island of Delos and it was led by Athens,

One of the most impressive korai from the archaic Acropolis. From the inscription on the statue base we learn that it was dedicated to the goddess by Nearchos (possibly the well-known vase-maker and vase-painter) as a 'first fruit' (aparche), an offering from his first earnings, and that it was the work of the sculptor Antenor. The monumental Antenor Kore, approximately 2 m tall, with her Ionic dress and inset rock crystal eyes (of which only a few fragments remain), is a characteristic example of archaic sculpture. 525-510 BC. Athens, Acropolis Museum, Level I, Archaic Gallery, Acr. 681.

with its mighty fleet. The decisive contribution of the skilled general Kimon, son of Miltiades, allowed the allies to enjoy many resounding military successes. Within a few years the Greek cities of Asia Minor had been liberated from the Persians and Athens had acquired immense power, prestige and wealth.

After Kimon's sudden death in 450 BC the fate of Athens passed to Pericles, the most charismatic of the Athenian leaders. It was under his leadership that the city reached its zenith. The signing of the Peace of Kallias in 449 BC put an end to the wars with the Persians, while the agreement for the cessation of hostilities with Sparta, the other great power of the day, temporarily averted the danger of conflict between the two cities. The Delian League had evolved into an Athenian hegemony. The democratic political system had reached its final form with the reforms of Ephialtes and Pericles. At the same time, thanks to the wonderful balance that democracy secured, philosophers, writers and artists flocked to the city from all parts of the Greek world. Athens, the spiritual capital of the era, opened new radical paths in all areas of art and thought.

Within such a climate of peace and prosperity, Pericles planned a grand building programme that would include works throughout Attica and, above all, the Acropolis. The Propylaia, the monumental entrance to the sacred area of the Acropolis, and the Parthenon, the magnificent marble temple that symbolised Athens during the classical period, were built. The expenses were huge. With the approval of the Athenian *deme*, however, Pericles was able to use some of the money from the League's treasury, which in 454 BC had been transferred from Delos to Athens.

The city's unprecedented flourishing came to a sudden end when, as a result of hostilities with Sparta, the fiercest war between Greeks yet broke out, the Peloponnesian War. This deadly conflict lasted for 27 years, from 431 to 404 BC, and ended with the pyrrhic victory of Sparta, as both combatants had essentially been destroyed. Even within the throes of war, however, the Athenians were able to proceed with the works of the Acropolis, building the Erechtheion and the small temple of Athena Nike.

The new century found Athens attempting to rise from the ashes. It is a fact that throughout the 4th century BC the city's cultural and artistic influence remained undiminished. New dedications were made on the Acropolis during this period, the works of fine artists such as Praxiteles and Leochares. Yet also at this time a new military power, Macedon, was attempting to gain the upper hand in Greece. The defeat of the Athenians at Chaironea in 338 BC under Philip II, king of the Macedonians, led to the city's cultural decline. Macedon's

Pericles, leader of the democratic faction, combined unique talents. An incorruptible and mild character, oratorical skills and a sharp intellect. His political and cultural work marked a whole era, Athens' most glorious and creative: the 'golden age'. Bust of Pericles, Roman copy of a lost original. London, British Museum.

dynamic policy was continued by Alexander the Great, Philip's son who succeeded his father in 336 BC. Two years later the young king was ready to undertake his legendary campaign, which led him to the depths of Asia and the creation of a vast empire. After his first major victory at the River Granicus in 334 BC, Alexander sent Persian shields, booty from the battle, to Athens, which were hung on the east side of the Parthenon.

Head of Alexander the Great. This portrait of the young king, one of the finest surviving, was perhaps produced after the battle of Chaironeia (338 BC), when Alexander visited Athens. It is believed to be either an original piece by the sculptor Leochares or a Roman copy of a work by Lysippus. Athens, Acropolis Museum, Level I, North section, Acr. 1331.

Hellenistic and Roman Eras

When Alexander died in 323 BC Athens was fought over by his competing successors. Even so, there was much building activity in the Hellenistic period, thanks to the benefactions of Alexander's successor kings. Antiochus Epiphanes, Attalus II and Eumenes II filled the city with stoas and gymnasia and the Acropolis with dedications.

The heyday of the Hellenistic kingdoms was followed by their

The Parthenon frieze, a work from the period 442-438 BC, is one of the most grandiose expressions of classical sculpture. On this block, which comes from the frieze on the east side of the temple, three Olympian gods, Poseidon, Apollo and Artemis, observe the Panathenaic procession. Apollo turns back to talk to Poseidon whilst his sister Artemis looks ahead. On the right we can see what remains of the figure of Aphrodite, goddess of beauty. Athens, Acropolis Museum, Parthenon Gallery.

gradual conquest by the Romans, which was fully accomplished by 30 BC with the annexation of Ptolemaic Egypt. In 86 BC the Roman general Sulla decided to punish the Athenians as they had sided with Mithridates, king of Pontus and enemy of Rome, and destroyed the city in a surprise attack.

Despite the Roman domination, however, Athens began to develop once more, in particular during the 2nd century AD. The city's borders were expanded and it was adorned with grand new buildings, such as the Library of Hadrian and the Odeion of Herodes Atticus. Its philosophical schools had won the admiration and support of eminent Romans and continued to offer knowledge to all those who sought it. The next watershed year in the city's history was AD 267, when it was literally razed to the ground by the Herulians, vicious invaders from the north. One view holds that the Parthenon then caught fire, resulting in the destruction of its roof and some interior damage. It is believed that repairs were undertaken a century or so later during the reign of the Roman emperor Julian.

Herodes Atticus (AD 101/2-177/8), scion of a wealthy Marathon family, fine orator, philosopher and one of the greatest benefactors of antiquity. His generosity gave Athens and many other cities of the then known world some of their finest buildings. Bust of Herodes Atticus, mid-2nd century AD. Athens, National Archaeological Museum.

Byzantine Era and Frankish Rule

With the birth of the Byzantine empire in the 4th century AD and the spread of Christianity, most ancient cities of Greece were relegated to becoming insignificant provincial centres. This happened with Athens too. In AD 529 the emperor Justinian closed the philosophical schools, thus extinguishing the last remnant of the city's former glory. In the meantime, the ancient temples were being gradually converted into churches since the early years of Christianity. The Parthenon also became a Christian church, being initially dedicated to the Holy Wisdom and later being renamed the Panagia, or Virgin, Atheniotissa.

The city experienced another brief revival in around AD 1000. This was when the Byzantine emperor Basil II repaired the Parthenon and decorated its interior with wall paintings. In the 12th century,

Barbarian raids marked the period of late antiquity and Byzantium. According ▶ to some historians the Parthenon was not set on fire in AD 267 by the Herulians but in AD 396 by the Visigoths, fanatical new Christian converts. Approximately two centuries later, Greece was traversed by Slavic tribes. They too may have passed through Athens and the Acropolis, which was now a castle. The treasure comprised of 234 gold coins mainly from the reigns of Heraklonas (AD 610-641) and Constans II (AD 641-668) and was discovered in 1876 in the Asclepeion on the south slope of the Acropolis. Acropolis Museum, Level I, North section.

▲ After the occupation of Athens by the Franks a very tall tower was built in the south section of the Propylaia, known as the 'Frankish Tower' or 'Koulas'. This tower, the main monument of the Frankish period in Athens, was demolished in 1874. North side of the Parthenon with the Frankish Tower. W. Cole, lithograph, 1835. From the book 'Select views of the remains of ancient monuments in Greece', (n.p., n.d).

Athens was pillaged once more, this time by the Saracen hordes. In his writings, the scholarly bishop Michael Choniates has preserved an evocative picture of the desolate image now presented by the once glorious city.

On 12 April 1204 Constantinople, capital of the Byzantine empire, was conquered by the armies of the Fourth Crusade. When the Crusaders divided the Byzantine territories between them Athens was given to Otto de la Roche, the son of a nobleman from Burgundy. The city then passed successively into the hands of other conquerors, such as the Catalans, the Florentine Acciajuoli family and the Venetians. During these years the Acropolis once more became a strong fortress, the Propylaia were converted into a palace for the foreign rulers, the Erechtheion became a residence and the Parthenon from an Orthodox church became a Roman Catholic church.

The Byzantines retook Constantinople in 1261. Athens was never able, however, to overthrow the Frank dynasty.

Ottoman Rule and the Greek War of Independence

The thousand-year history of the Byzantine empire came to a definitive end in May 1453, when Constantinople fell into the hands of the Ottoman Turks. Three years later, in 1456, the Turks entered Athens. During the almost four centuries of Ottoman rule, the image of the city changed once more. The Acropolis was filled with houses. The Parthenon was converted into a mosque and a minaret erected in its southwest corner. The harem of the Turkish garrison leader was installed in the Erechtheion, whilst the administrative centre and market, the Bazaar, were developed in the lower town around the Roman market and the Library of Hadrian.

Despite the passage of so many centuries the Parthenon had been altered little, at least externally. Indeed, when Charles-Marie-François Olier, the marquis de Nointel and French king Louis XIV's ambassador to Constantinople, visited Athens in 1674 one of the members of his retinue, the young painter Jacques Carrey, made detailed drawings of many of the temple's sculptures. His work was destined to be invaluable. Thirteen years later, during the Venetian-Ottoman wars, the Venetians, led by Francesco Morosini, besieged the Acropolis. Disaster was looming. On 26 September 1687, a Venetian shell fell onto the Parthenon, which the Turks were using as a gunpowder store, and a large section of it was blown away. As they left in 1688 the Venetians attempted to remove the horses from the west pediment of the dilap-

The small Ionic temple of Athena Nike was demolished in 1686, by the Turks who were at war with the Venetians, and its building material reused in the construction of a rampart in front of the Propylaia. The Turkish rampart was demolished between 1834 and 1838 and the first restoration of the ancient temple began, a task which was completed after 1844. The temple was taken down before the Second World War and reconstructed. Watercolour by C.F. Werner, 1877. Athens, Benaki Museum.

Following the instructions of General Makriyiannis, a fighter of 1821, the folk artist Panagiotis Zographos produced twenty-four paintings of battles, including one with the subject of the siege of the Acropolis by Kioutachis. Siege of Athens in 1827. Thoughts of I. Makriyiannis, 1836. By P. Zographos, copy by D. Zographos. Athens, Gennadios Library.

idated temple and take them with them. The precious sculptures, however, fell to the ground and broke into pieces. In the next century, especially from the mid-century onwards, Greece became a favoured destination for wealthy Europeans collecting works of art – and the Acropolis was no exception. The greatest blow came from the Briton Thomas Bruce, seventh Earl of Elgin, who removed a large section of the Parthenon sculptures (56 of the 97 surviving blocks of the frieze, 19 figures from the pediments and 15 metopes from the south side), as well as sections from other ancient monuments. But this was not all. As these marbles were being removed the adjacent blocks also suffered irreversible damage, whilst Elgin's ships were so overloaded with these invaluable sculptures that two were shipwrecked: thankfully the cargo of the 'Mentor' (17 crates of sculptures), which sank near Kythera, was successfully raised to the surface by divers from Kalymnos and Symi. Elgin's collection was sold to the British government in 1816, which offered them to the British Museum, where they have been housed until this day.

The most important event in the history of modern Hellenism, the Greek War of Independence, broke out in March of 1821. Almost from the outset Athens, and the Acropolis in particular, was a battlefield between Greeks and Turks. On 10 June 1822, after a fierce siege, the Greeks took the sacred rock and liberated the city. In a few years, this situation had been completely overturned, when, in the summer of 1826 the Turkish army, commanded by Mustafa Reshid Pasha or Kutahye, once more laid siege to the Acropolis. The Greeks who had defended it handed the Acropolis over to the Turks in May 1827.

The Modern Era

Despite the difficulties encountered, the revolution ended favourably for the Greeks, and the independent Greek state was recognised in February 1830. Its first king was Otto, son of Ludwig of Bavaria, who arrived in Greece in 1833. It was on his decision in late 1834 that Athens became the capital of the newly-formed state. This led to a building boom which, as the years went by, filled the city with wonderful new buildings inspired by the two great trends in European architecture of the 19th century, neoclassicism and romanticism. Efforts also began to preserve and showcase the monuments of the Acropolis. Excavations in 1885-1890 brought to light, amongst other things, the pits and the fragments of the temples and the sculptures of the archaic period, thus providing the Acropolis Museum with some of its most splendid exhibits. Also in the late 19th century systemat-

ic, large-scale reconstruction work started, continuing almost without interruption until the Second World War.

Soon, however, new dangers began to threaten the Acropolis, such as corrosion of the marble caused by atmospheric pollution and rusting of the iron joints used initially in the reconstruction. In response, the interdisciplinary Committee for the Preservation of the Acropolis Monuments was founded in 1975 with the aim of studying and implementing large-scale stabilisation and reconstruction projects, an activity which is still being continued by the competent authorities. In recent years the Unification of the Archaeological Sites of Athens has been programmed, and as the studies and the works proceed we are forming a more complete image of the ancient city.

As for the masterpieces on the sacred rock, they are now housed, after a long wait, in the fitting new Museum, an impressive building that opens a contemporary window onto the charming world of the ancient Acropolis.

The Old Military Hospital at Makriyianni, one of the new capital's first public buildings, was constructed in 1834-1836 by the German W. von Weiler. The preserved 'Weiler building', as it is known today, is located directly next to the Acropolis Museum and is home to the Centre for Acropolis Studies. Athens, National Historical Museum.

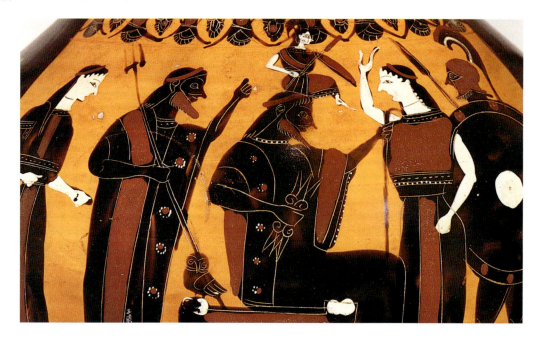

Vase-painting depicting the birth of Athena. Athena jumps fully armed from the head of Zeus, who sits holding a sceptre in his left hand and a thunderbolt in his right, surprising the gods present. Paris, Musée du Louvre.

MYTHOLOGICAL TIMES

Athena was the honoured goddess on the Acropolis, venerable daughter of Zeus, lord of gods and men, and of Metis, goddess of prudence. As the ancient Greeks narrated, when Metis was pregnant with Athena, Zeus received a prophecy that his beloved would bring into the world first a daughter and then a son who would seize power from him. In order for this prophecy never to come true, he decided to swallow Metis. She was already pregnant with Athena, however, who then grew in her father's head. When the time came for her birth, Zeus ordered the Titan Prometheus or, according to some versions, the god of metallurgy Hephaestus, to split open his head with an axe. And then, in front of the other gods, who were stunned, the new goddess sprung out fully armed - the goddess of wisdom, a peaceful goddess, patron of artisans and a goddess with a marked military nature. One of her leading symbols was the owl, which graced the coins of ancient Athens.

For the Athenians there was yet another important dimension to Athena, that of Polias, or the protector of their city. Indeed, in order to win this title she had to compete against Poseidon, the god of the sea, who also wanted to make the beautiful city his own. In order to put an end to the dispute, the two gods agreed to offer a gift each. Whoever, in the judgement of the other gods, offered the better gift would be the winner. The contest took place on the Acropolis rock.

Poseidon first struck his tripod to the ground and water immediately gushed out. With a gesture from Athena, the world's first olive tree sprouted. Without a second thought, the gods declared Zeus' daughter the victor and, since then, the city has borne her name.

Associated with the dispute between Poseidon and Athena was king Kekrops, a very ancient figure in Attica, whom the people believed to be an autochthon, that is born of the earth, and to have a double form: human from the waist up and snake from the waist down. Attic tradition holds that Kekrops built a wall around the Acropolis rock, made laws and gave order to the relationships between humans by teaching them monogamy. He brought the alphabet to Athens and was even present during the contest between the two gods on the Acropolis, with some saying he himself was the judge.

Attica has a rich mythology, with many tales referring to the birth of the city of Athens, the region's demographic composition, its social and political institutions, forms of public worship and the relationship of the Athenian state with other polities. The protagonists were gods and kings, such as Erichthonius, Pandion, Erechtheus and Theseus. Theseus was Athens' greatest hero, killing the fearsome man-eating Minotaur on Crete and being responsible for the 'synoecism', whereby all the inhabitants of Attica were brought together in Athena's city of Athens.

According to the myth, the Athenians were at one point obliged to send seven young men and seven young women to Crete each year as food for the Minotaur, a fearsome creature with the body of a man and the head of a bull. Theseus, the greatest Athenian hero, was finally able to kill him. In the depiction Theseus drags along the dying Minotaur. Next to him, Athena supports the hero. Inside of a red-figure kylix, ca 420 BC. Madrid, Museo Arqueológico Nacional.

Upon the Acropolis, within the silent recess of this place emerging from prehistory, rises a language, full of passions, almost a cry, a brief din, whole, violent, compact, voluminous, piercing, sharp, decisive: the marble of the temples carries the human voice.

Le Corbusier, 1935

THE ACROPOLIS

THE ACROPOLIS

The dominant deity of the Acropolis rock throughout antiquity was Athena, who was worshipped in a variety of aspects: as the city patron Athena Polias in the Erechtheion; as Athena Pallas and Parthenos with her military aspect in the Parthenon; as Athena Nike in the small temple of the same name; as Athena Ergani, patron of the arts and artisans, perhaps in the small sanctuary located in the north wing of the Parthenon; and as Athena Hygieia near the Propylaia. Bronze statue of Athena, perhaps by the sculptor Euphranos, ca 350 BC. Piraeus, Archaeological Museum.

The word Acropolis is a compound word made up of the words 'akra' and 'polis', that is the highest (akra) point of the city (polis). Acropolises, i.e. fortified crags or citadels, existed in many areas of Greece from the prehistoric period. One such citadel from this early period was the Acropolis of Athens. Over time, however, its role changed and it gradually became the city's main religious centre and home to some of the masterpieces of ancient Greek architecture and sculpture.

The two historical periods that left their mark most indelibly on the sacred rock were the archaic and the classical periods. The Acropolis of the earlier archaic period was stormed by the Persians in 480 BC. After this, tradition holds, and a little before the battle of Plataea in 479 BC, the Greeks vowed to leave their sanctuaries in ruins so that they would always remember the barbarity of the Persian invaders. As a result, when the Athenians returned victorious to their city they did not start to rebuild their temples. Only the 'old temple' of Athena on the Acropolis was repaired, seemingly in makeshift fashion, in order to house the goddess's *xoanon*, an ancient wooden cult statue which the Athenians considered to be *diipetes*, that is heaven-sent and not made by human hand.

Approximately thirty years after the Persian Wars, things changed. Pericles desired to see Athens as the most brilliant city in Greece and thus initiated an extremely well thought out building programme, which was ratified by the Athenians. This programme included large works on the Acropolis. General supervision was assigned to the gifted sculptor Phidias, a close friend of Pericles described as the 'overseer of everything' by the ancient writer Plutarch (c. AD 50-120). He was not alone, however, and alongside side him worked the finest and most innovative architects and craftsmen of the era. A team that in a few years designed and constructed buildings unsurpassed in size and grace. Pericles, the man who had envisioned an Athens that was strong, democratic and grand, died in the terrible plague that swept through the city in 429 BC. The building programme on the Acropolis continued after his death, however.

The limestone Acropolis rock, 156 metres high, from the west. In front are the Propylaia and the temple of Athena Nike, to the left the Erechtheion and to the right the Parthenon. The Athenians called the Acropolis the 'great rocky eminence of Pallas'. The term Acropolis was used officially for the first time in the early 4th century BC.

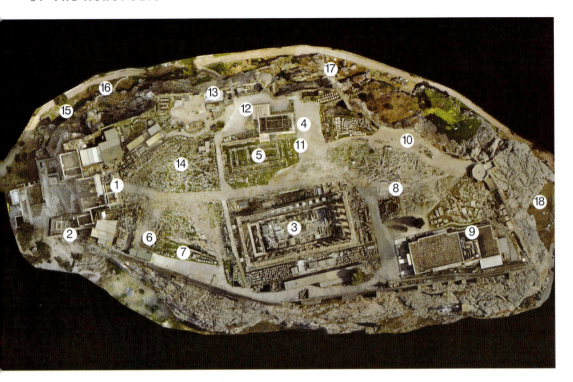

Orthophoto mosaic plan of the Acropolis rock. It was produced by the Acropolis Restoration Service as part of the Development of Geographical Information Systems for the Acropolis programme, with funding from the "Information Society" Operational Programme.

Reaching the sacred rock

The west side of the Acropolis, the least formidable of all, always provided the main access to the summit of the sacred rock although its layout differed, of course, from era to era. During the Mycenaean period there was a narrow pathway that started from the south, ascended the west slope and ended at the fortified entrance to the Acropolis. Later, during the reorganisation of the Panathenaia (566 BC), a large ramp was built for the ascent of the grand procession during the festival. It was approximately 80 metres long and 10 metres wide and led directly from the western foot of the rock to the entrance to the sanctuary. When the Propylaia were built the archaic entranceway was extended in width to occupy the whole area between the lateral wings of the new building.

The old Propylaia

From as early as the Mycenaean period the main entrance to the Acropolis had been located on the west side of the rock, at approximately the same point as the Propylaia. An early propylon gate, simple

Mnesikles' Propylaia, a later building featuring many architectural innovations. The access route leading to the Propylaia in the classical period was replaced by a monumental stairway during the reign of the Roman emperor Claudius (AD 52). In the 19th century a section of the stairway was restored, only to be removed again in 1959 so that the paved pathway that still serves visitors today could be constructed.

Reconstruction of the back of the Propylaia and the sanctuary of Athena, with its valuable votives (G.P. Stevens).
In the background to the left is the colossal bronze statue of Athena Promachos, a statue so tall that, as tradition holds, the tip of the spear and the crest of the helmet could be seen kilometres away. It is said that with the establishment of Christianity it was taken to Constantinople, where it was destroyed by the crowds a little before the Crusaders occupied the city (AD 1204).

in design and with a different orientation from the Propylaia, was constructed here perhaps in the 6th century BC. This propylon gate, which it is believed also underwent a building phase in 490-480 BC, must have been destroyed by the Persians (480 BC) and been repaired or rebuilt as part of the post-war fortification programme.

The Propylaia

The monumental Propylaia from Pericles' time was erected on the site of an older, simpler propylon gate. Its construction started in 437 BC and stopped in 432 BC, perhaps due to the imminent outbreak of the Peloponnesian Wars, or perhaps for other reasons. Even though the initial design was not completed, the Propylaia of Pericles could not but be worthy of the Parthenon. Its architect Mnesikles ingen-

The word 'propylaia' (singular: 'propylon'), is used to describe the monumental entrance-way to a particular space, sacred or otherwise, or a building.

East view of the central section of the Propylaia. In the modern period the buildings of the sacred rock have suffered severed corrosion due to rusting of the iron used in the restoration work in the first half of the 20th century. These problems have been resolved in the past few decades and the monuments are now conserved and restored on the basis of expert studies and the contemporary restoration principles and philosophy. View of the Acropolis before modern restoration work began.

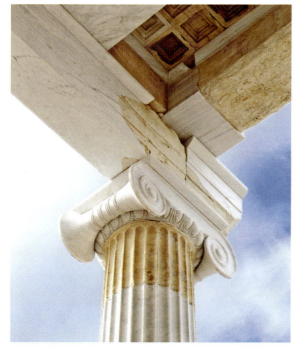

Detail of the restored roof of the central section of the Propylaia. The column capital in the photograph is a precise copy of the column capitals created twenty-five centuries ago by Mnesikles and his team.

View of the restored roof of the central section of the Propylaia. In keeping with contemporary restoration principles as many ancient pieces as possible were used in the restoration of the Acropolis monuments, although only once their exact original positions had been identified. Modern-day craftsmen filled in the gaps, where necessary, with marble cut in such a way as to match the fracture surface of the ancient piece.

iously approached the problems posed by the limited space and the lie of the land. His creation, grand and harmonic, constructed almost completely of white Pentelic marble, is an ideal prelude to the architectural structures within the sacred space.

The Propylaia complex is comprised of a central building flanked by two wings, the northwest and the southwest. On the facade of the central building rise six Doric columns placed at equal distances with the exception of the two central ones which are further apart from each other. This larger opening facilitated the entry of the horses and animals in the Panathenaic procession. Two colonnades were built perpendicular to the facade, each with three slim Ionic columns. The back section of the central building is at a higher level to the front section. In order to counter the difference in height between these two spaces, which communicate via five doors, different roofs were used, painted inside with a deep blue and decorated with gold metal stars. The back face of the central building has six Doric columns, as does the front.

The northwest wing of the Propylaia included the space known as the Pinakotheke, a name derived from a detail provided by the 2nd-century AD traveller Pausanias that its walls were adorned with paintings (on canvas or wall paintings). A small Doric stoa was built in front of it, with three columns: it is believed that there was a couch here where visitors could rest. The second wing, in the southwest, has a different form as its design was influenced by the presence of the venerable remains of the Mycenaean wall, parts of which still survive, and the sanctuary of Athena Nike. There is thus only one stoa, corresponding to that in the north wing. Scholars believe that, in the first plans, the architect of the Propylaia had foreseen the construction of corresponding stoas on the east side as well, although these were never constructed.

The pedestal of Agrippa

A tall pedestal of blue-grey Hymettus marble survives in front of the Pinakotheke, atop of which stood a four-horse chariot in honour of Eumenes II the king of Pergamon after his victory in the Panathenaic Games of 178 BC. Later, at the end of the 1st century BC, the same monument was dedicated to a Roman benefactor of the city, Marcus Vipsanius Agrippa.

As we know from the ancient sources, there was a herm within the space of the Propylaia, a bust, that is, of the god Hermes atop a square column, which became known as the Hermes Propylaios and was a work of Alcamenes, a famous student of Phidias. Copy of the Hermes Propylaios, 1st c. AD. Athens, Acropolis Museum, Level I, West section, Acr. 2281.

The pedestal of Agrippa and the northwest edge of the Propylaia. From 1205 to 1456 the Propylaia had been converted into a fortified palace that housed the Latin dukes, whilst in the Turkish period gunpowder was stored in one section of it. In the mid-17th century a bolt of lightening – or an exploding cannon, according to another tradition – blew up the gunpowder store, destroying a large part of the building.

The Beulé Gate

After the destruction of Athens by the Herulians in AD 267 the Athenians renovated the fortifications of the Acropolis, especially on the exposed western side. Using as their building material pieces from the older buildings, especially the choregic monument of Nikias that had been located on the south slope of the rock, they constructed a gate framed by two strong towers. This was the Beulé Gate, located directly below the Propylaia, and which was named after Charles Beulé, the French archaeologist who excavated it in the middle of the nineteenth century.

The temple of Athena Nike

From the tall tower of the small Ionic temple of Athena Nike one could gaze out towards the sea. It was from here, so the myth goes, that Aegeus, father of Theseus, threw himself when he saw his son's boat from afar, returning from Crete with black sails and thus leading him to believe that Theseus had been killed by the Minotaur.
This space, however, had cult attributes from very ancient times and a small sanctuary in the form of a double conch has been found on the west side of the Mycenaean tower that protected the entrance to the Acropolis in that far-gone age.

To the southwest of the Propylaia, on top of a Mycenaean defence wall renovated in the classical period, stands the temple of Athena Nike. This is where Athena was worshipped with the epithet Nike, Victory. The temple that the visitor will see today is the successor of earlier ones, also dedicated to Athena Nike. Studies have shown that a wooden temple stood here in the mid-6th century BC, which was destroyed during the Persian raid in 480 BC. The *eschara*, or hearth, that was found here, a type of altar which it is believed was used as the base of the wooden cult statue of Athena, is also believed to date to the same period of the mid-6th century BC. After the Persian wars, in around 468 BC, the ruined wooden temple was replaced by a poros (limestone) one, in front of which was built a poros altar. A little later the tower and temple of Athena Nike were radically renovated.

The construction of the new temple was assigned to the architect Kallikrates in 449/8 BC, although work was not completed until much later, in around 425 BC. During the new construction the old Mycenaean tower was furnished with new poros walls, built with isodomic masonry, thus expanding its dimensions. In

The Ionic temple of Athena Nike from the west. Excavations of the earth fills from the classical tower revealed, amongst other things, the remains of an earlier temple from the time of Kimon and sections of a dedicatory inscription to Athena Nike from the altar dating to around the mid-6th century BC. It should be noted that the cult was not limited to Athena: prior to the classical period sanctuaries of the Graces and Hecate Epipyrgidia stood at the spot in front of the sanctuary of Athena Nike.

The east pediment, upper section of the columns on the east side and a section of the frieze (copy) of the temple of Athena Nike. As with the other monuments on the Acropolis, the earlier restoration programme has proved problematic. The use of iron joints caused cracks in the marble whilst the setting of architectural pieces in the wrong positions distorted the temple's geometry, resulting in the east side deviating by 4.5 cm. The modern restoration of the temple, based on a thorough study of the building, began in 2000. A new feature is the reconstruction, from fragments, of part of the east pediment and a small section of the west pediment.

contrast with the tower, the new temple was built in marble: a small, elegant, amphiprostyle temple, with four columns at its front and rear facades. It does not have a pronaos, whilst its cella (the main temple), where the sidewalls end in antae, is open, i.e. without a wall containing a door. Only two pillars are flanked by antae and were connected to them with a metal railing, thus preventing access to the interior.

The temple's sculptural decoration is also of particular interest. One section of the delicate frieze, decorated with relief images, is to be found in the British Museum, and the remainder in the Acropolis Museum. The gods of Olympus were represented on the east side, whilst the other sides featured battle scenes between Greeks and Persians and also between Greeks. Relief representations also adorned the pediments, which it is believed had as their subject matter the Amazonomachy (battle between Athenians and Amazons) and the Gigantomachy (battle between gods and Giants). A parapet made of marble slabs was placed along the edge of the bastion on three sides, for the protection of the pilgrims. Wonderful winged Nikes in relief adorned the inner surface, some decorating trophies, others leading oxen to sacrifice, and Athena with her weapons seated in amongst them.

The cult statue of Athena Nike stood within the temple, holding a helmet and a pomegranate. The traveller Pausanias (2nd c. AD), believing that the temple was dedicated to winged Nike, calls it the temple of Athena Apteros (Wingless Athena) as the statue did not have wings. It is said that the Athenians had represented Athena thus so that she would never fly far from Athens.

The sanctuary of Aphrodite Pandemos

The sanctuary of Aphrodite Pandemos, patron of the *deme*, is situated near the bastion of the temple of Athena Nike. As Pausanias informs us, statues by fine artists had been dedicated in the goddess's sanctuary. The sanctuary of Aphrodite Pandemos must have been located amongst other ancient sanctuaries and the two niches that survive in the west wall of the bastion of Athena Nike may have had a cult function.

Earlier Parthenons

The ancient Greeks believed in the sanctity of certain places, and for this reason would always build their temples on the same spots. Archaeological studies have shown that on the site where the Parthenon was later built, a large poros Doric temple had been built in around 570 BC. This has been identified with the famous Hekatompedon, the temple

Four-horse chariot from a metope attributed to the Hekatompedon and produced in around 570 BC. Initially, the horses were located in front of a plaque upon which the charioteer also appeared, either in relief or painted. Athens, Acropolis Museum, Level I, Archaic Gallery, Acr. 575+.

The Parthenon from the southwest, with the Erechtheion in the background. The huge, luxurious temple of the goddess Athena has been studied and restored systematically in recent years. Despite the large number of studies that has already been published on the famous temple and the many researchers involved, the Parthenon still has surprises in store for those studying it.

measuring one hundred Attic feet in length and which is mentioned in ancient inscriptions. It is believed that the large poros sculptures and architectural pieces found during the late-19th-century excavations at the top of the Acropolis originated from this temple, as did some pieces subsequently built into the Propylaia and north wall.

Later, after the battle of Marathon (490 BC), construction began on a new marble temple, on the site of the earlier poros one. Work on the new temple, dubbed the Pre-Parthenon, had progressed as far as the first column drums when the Acropolis was razed by the Persians (480 BC). After the second great Persian campaign against Greece, the Athenians reused some of the architectural pieces during construction of the north wall of the Acropolis. Other spolia were later incorporated into the splendid classical Parthenon.

The Parthenon

Athena's multi-dimensional personality has furnished her with numerous epithets, such as Nike (the victor), Ergane (she who taught men crafts) and Promachos (protector in battles). She was also sometimes known simply as Parthenos (virgin), and for this reason the great temple built in her honour on the Acropolis in the mid-5th century BC was named the Parthenon.

The architects of the temple were Iktinos and Kallikratis, whilst Phidias also had a particularly important role in its design. Living in a city that overflowed with new intellectual currents, these great creators were freed from tradition, although without ignoring it completely, and were able to open new roads. Through the amalgamation of the familiar elements of Doric and Ionian architecture a new form emerged, which we could call Attic. The Parthenon and the other artistic creations of the 5th century BC expressed in their own language the new intellectual climate of the day, an intellectual climate that led to the birth of tragedy and democracy.

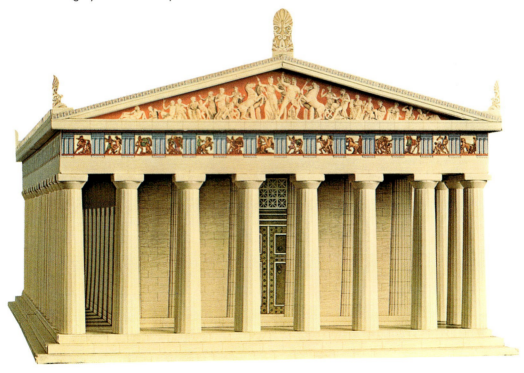

Reconstruction of the west side of the temple that the Athenians dedicated to the Parthenos (Virgin), Pallas Athena, the goddess in her military aspect. The name Parthenon, which means 'house of the Parthenos', was initially used for a section of the temple and in the 4th century was expanded to cover the whole building. In the 5th century BC the Parthenon was referred to as the 'megas neos' (large temple) or the 'Hekatompedos neos'.

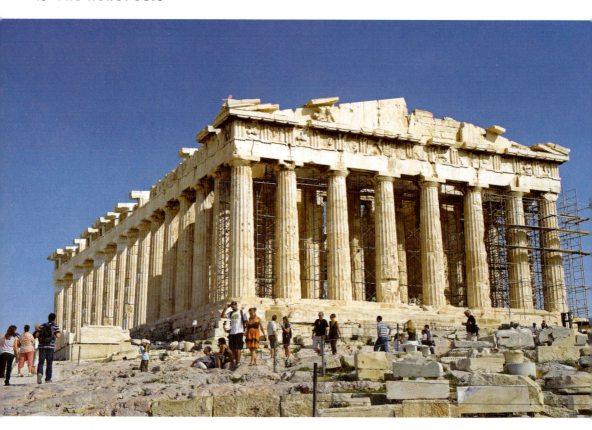

The Parthenon from the north-west. The grand classical temple was built upon the limestone foundations over which construction of the 'Proparthenon' had begun. Because, however, the Parthenon was a little shorter and much wider than this temple a section of the foundations in the east have remained unused whilst, by contrast, another zone was added in the north. Research has shown that the temple's north wing had incorporated into it a pre-classical temple and its altar, dedicated perhaps to Athena Ergani.

The speed with which the Parthenon was built is impressive. Construction started in 447 BC and it was inaugurated in 438 BC, although the pedimental sculptures were completed six years later, in 432 BC. It is even more remarkable if one considers that the Parthenon was the largest Doric temple in the ancient Greek world, and the only one to be built almost completely in marble and with relief representations on all its metopes. Its uniqueness, however, is not apparent only in its size or richness, both products of the city's economic prosperity. It is primarily apparent in the details that turned lifeless blocks of marble into a unified whole that pulsates with life.

The building's dimensions were determined by the ratio 4:9. This ratio was the basis of the diameter of the columns to the intercolumniations (the spacing between the axes of two successive columns), the height of the whole temple in relation to its width, and the width of the main temple in relation to its length. This absolute symmetry did not, however, produce a composition that was heavy and static, since those elements that had to be vertical, such as the columns and the walls, externally lean slightly inwards. The temple was thus pyramidical and, as a result, had an upward motion. In addition to these

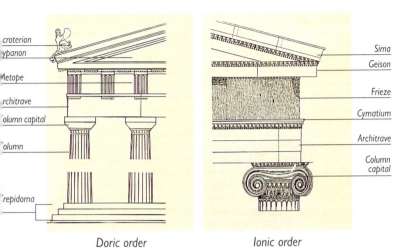

croterion
ypanon
Metope
rchitrave
olumn capital
olumn
repidoma

Sima
Geison
Frieze
Cymatium
Architrave
Column capital

Doric order   Ionic order

The Doric and the Ionic were the two main architectural orders of ancient Greece. The former, which was simpler and more austere, prevailed on mainland Greece. The latter, born on the Aegean islands and the Asia Minor coast, was lighter, with a great love of decorative features. The Athenians, although of Ionian origin, made almost exclusive use of the Doric order until the mid-5th century, when the Ionic order discreetly started to make its appearance on the new buildings of the Acropolis.

inclines, certain other 'optical refinements', as they are known, were applied to the Parthenon, such as curves and *entasis*. The stylobate, for example, the surface upon which the columns stood, is not absolutely horizontal but curves in the middle. The columns also have *entasis*, bulging at about one-third of their height. Moreover, the corner columns are also slightly thicker than the others, so as not to lose volume when viewed against the clear blue sky. All these and countless other details do not only give the temple movement and vibrancy, they are testimony to the astonishing precision with which it was built. We only need consider that, because of the inclinations and curves, each marble block has its own unique shape and individual position in the whole.

Externally, the Parthenon has Doric columns along all its sides, eight

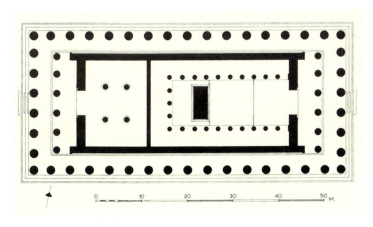

0   10   20   30   40   50 M.

Plan of the Parthenon (J. Travlos). The temple was peripteral, that is with columns externally on all its sides, and it was built over a crepidoma with three very high steps. To reach the temple pilgrims used the stairs in between the east and west facades. It should be noted that in antiquity religious rituals took place in the open, around altars; the temple gates were opened only during festivals. The dimensions of the stylobate (30.880 x 69.503 m) are regarded as the dimensions of the whole building. Its unusually large width was due to the large chryselephantine statue of Athena that adorned its interior.

The northwest corner of the Parthenon entablature, the section between the column capitals and the pediment, as it survives today. Next to it, a reconstruction of the same corner as it was in antiquity. The corner metopes, the marble acroteria, with their relief palmettes above two volutes and which adorned the short sides of the temple, and an ornamental lion's head can be seen. The gable roof was made of marble tiles supported on a frame of cypress wood.

View of the columns of the north side of the Parthenon, a building constructed with inconceivable precision. One of the issues that has been much discussed is that of the temple's construction details, in particular its so-called 'refinements' (curvatures, entasis, gradients, different thickness of the corner columns). According to the researchers, these 'refinements' were ideas that had been applied on older temples, whilst on the Parthenon they were used in a particularly impressive way. The columns, for example: their clever design and excellently applied curvature express their strength. In other words, their ability to lift the temple structure makes visual their internal strength.

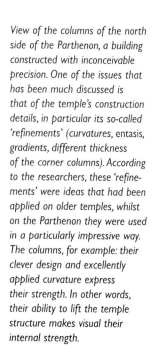

Reconstruction of the chryselephantine statue of Athena. Phidias's masterpiece was comprised of a wooden inner core that had been dressed in ivory and gold. The gold leaves (approximately 1,140 kilos) were arranged in such a way that, when Phidias was accused by his enemies of having stolen some of the gold, the leaves were removed and weighed and, as their weight was exactly as it should be, the artist was proved innocent.

The east side of the Parthenon. The large rectangular openings that can be seen on the architrave were used to hold the Persian shields that 'Alexander and the Greeks minus the Spartans' dedicated on the Acropolis, after the battle at the River Granicus (334 BC). Here, on the east side, was the entrance of the temple in antiquity; in Christian times, however, it was moved to the west. The large conch of the holy bema was developed in the east.

on the narrow sides and seventeen on the long. Inside the perimeter colonnade the building is hexastyle and amphiprostyle, i.e. with six columns at the front and six at the back, and is comprised of a pronaos, the main temple (cella) and the opisthonaos. The cella was divided into two chambers, which did not intercommunicate. Four Ionic columns supported the roof of the smaller, west chamber. Valuable items and the city's money were stored here, just as they were in other parts of the temple. The famous chryselephantine statue of Athena was located in the west chamber, in front of a two-floor Doric colonnade in the shape of a Π. This towering statue, approximately twelve metres high and set on a pedestal, represented the goddess as upright and armed. She wore a richly-decorated Attic helmet, a Doric *peplos* and on her breast the aegis (protective goatskin breastplate) with a Gorgon's head (a mythical monster who turned all those who looked at her to stone). Her left hand rested on her shield, within which her sacred snake lay sleeping, whilst in her right hand she held a Nike. One tradition holds that Phidias' gold-and-ivory masterpiece was taken to Constantinople in the 5th century AD, after which all traces of it were lost.

The sculptural decoration of the Parthenon

The image of the temple is completed by its sculptured decoration, born of the far-reaching imagination of Phidias and his students. In order to form a more vivid picture of their beauty, we must bear in mind that the ancient Greeks used bright colours on their architectural pieces and sculptures, primarily red, blue and gold. The traces of colour that have survived on the Parthenon lead us to believe that its painted decoration must have been exceptionally lavish. At certain points bronze attachments were inserted, as can be ascertained from the drill holes on the hands of the horsemen, for example, who held bridles, and the rust that is visible at various points on the temple's frieze. Many of the wonderful sculptures of the Parthenon have been lost. We are still able to reconstruct its iconographic wealth from the pieces that remain and which are housed in the Acropolis Museum and the British Museum, as well as from the drawings of the Flemish painter Jacques Carrey.

A total of 92 metopes were positioned above the outer colonnade, all decorated with relief representations. On the east side, the 5th-century BC artists represented the Gigantomachy (the confronta-

According to the myth, Perithous, the king of the Lapiths, invited the Centaurs, creatures that were human from the waist up and horse from the waist down, to his wedding to the beautiful Deidameia. The Centaurs, however, became drunk and attacked the bride and the other Lapiths. This battle, which became known as the Centauromachy and in which Perithous's friend Theseus participated, ended with a Lapith victory. Metope with the Centauromachy, from the south side of the Parthenon. London, British Museum.

Reconstruction of the east pediment of the Parthenon. In the centre is Zeus, seated on the throne, with Athena standing next to him fully armed, having just sprung from her father's head. Near her stands the god Hephaestus who, according to myth, split open Zeus's head with an axe so that the goddess could be born. Other gods can be seen to the right and left. In the left corner of the pediment the god Helios rises from the sea (only the god himself and the four horses who drew his chariot can be seen), whilst to the right the moon-goddess Selene sinks, indicating that the birth took place at dawn.

Reconstruction of the west pediment of the Parthenon. The dominant figures here are Athena and Poseidon. Next to them are their chariots, with the charioteers Nike in one and Amphitrite, wife of Poseidon, in the other. The central scene is flanked by gods and other mythical figures, such as Kekrops, king of Athens, and his daughter Pandrosos. At the corner of the pediment appears a river god, perhaps Ilissos or Eridanus, half-reclining, and in the other corner the spring Kallirhoe with a river god, perhaps Ilissos, next to her.

Etymologically, *aetoma* (pediment) derives from the word *aetos* (eagle). The shape of the pediment is indeed reminiscent of an eagle with its wings spread. Of the approximately fifty larger than life-size statues that adorned the two pediments of the Parthenon only eleven have survived. Most are located in the British Museum, whilst the rest are in the Acropolis Museum.

tion between gods and Giants), on the west the Amazonomachy (battle between Athenians and Amazons), on the north the fall of Troy and in the south, with the exception of the middle metopes which feature a variety of subjects, the Centauromachy (clash between the Lapiths of Thessaly and the Centaurs). The subjects represented on the metopes, inspired by the world of myth, symbolise the overcoming of the forces of evil by the forces of good.

Phidias' vision was not, however, confined to traditional mythological scenes. Alongside them he also wished to extol Athenian democracy and, by extension, peaceful creativity. He overturned what was known and established and chose to render a living and familiar image on the marble: the people of Athens during one of their most joyful events, the procession of the Great Panathenaia. During the Great Panathenaia, celebrated in the third year of every Olympiad, music and

Section of the west pediment and the west metopes of the Parthenon, which were dedicated to the Amazonomachy. In the pediment, which featured the conflict between Poseidon and Athena for guardianship of Athens, we can see the group of the mythical Athenian king Kekrops and his daughter Pandrosos (copy). Although the pediments of the Parthenon were pillaged by Lord Elgin's team, led by the Italian painter Giovanni Battista Lusieri, this group remained in its place. Lusieri wrongly believed that this was a Roman piece portraying the emperor Hadrian and his wife Sabina.

Section of the east metopes and the west pediment of the Parthenon, with the horse and carriage of Helios and the half-reclining figure of Dionysius from the scene of Athena's birth. Beneath the much destroyed metopes of the Gigantomachy can be seen a series of openings, some large and with groups of smaller ones in between them. From the former were once hung the shields sent by Alexander the Great from Persia, whilst on the smaller were fixed, in imperial Roman times, the bronze letters of an inscription in honour of the emperor Nero, who visited Greece in AD 66.

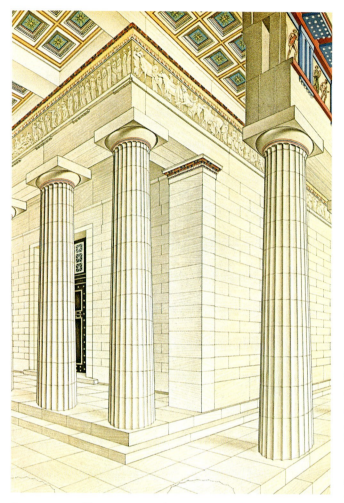

Reconstruction of the northeast side of the pronaos and section of the frieze (Greek = zoophoros, a composite word formed from the noun zoe *[life] and the verb* phero *[to bear]) of the Parthenon. This famous frieze has a length of 160 m and a height of around 1 m. It was decorated with approximately 380 human figures and over 220 animal figures, mostly horses. The frieze was located high up, where there was no light, and would thus have been difficult to see. Even so, it is one of the most brilliant masterpieces of ancient Greek art. Here we should note that, according to a particularly interesting new theory, the Parthenon also had a second Ionic frieze, which is unfortunately now lost to us today.*

sporting contests, torch races and many other events were held. The most sacred part of the festival was the official procession, which started at the Kerameikos and made its way to the Acropolis to present the goddess with offerings, primarily her sacred *peplos* cloak, hanging like a mast from a ship on wheels. The priests would dress the ancient wooden cult statue of Athena, believed to have fallen from the heavens, and which was woven by Athenian maidens.

In order to represent the Panathenaic procession, Phidias resorted to a radical solution. He added an Ionian element to the Doric building – a continuous frieze running above the colonnade of the pronaos, the opisthonaos and high on the walls of the cella. Upon this frieze were carved young horsemen, hoplites, elders, lyre-players and flute-players, youths with pitchers full of water, others who led animals to the slaughter or carried trays of sweetmeats, maidens and masters of ceremony. This lively, proud procession ended on the east side of the frieze, where the seated gods of Olympus received the sacrifices intended for Athena.

The cycle of the Parthenon decoration was completed by the colossal compositions on the pediments, unrivalled in conception and execution. The west pediment showed the dispute between Athena and Poseidon, and the east pediment the birth of the goddess from the head of Zeus. This scene was of particular significance for the Athenians as the birth of Athena, who in a sense represented the diving aspect of the city, symbolised the dawn of a new era for Athens.

The Erechtheion

To the north of the Parthenon stands the Erechtheion, the building which housed the wooden *diiepetes* ('heaven-sent') cult statue of Athena, for which the new *peplos* of the Panathenaic festival was destined. The temple was not initially called the Erechtheion and this name is only mentioned by the traveller Pausanias in the 2nd century AD in relation to the mythical king Erechtheus who appears over time to have become identified with Poseidon. For the ancient Athenians, this was the 'old temple' or the 'city temple where the ancient statue is'.

This complex building was initially dedicated to Athena Polias, the protector of the city, and to Poseidon/Erechtheus. It also enclosed, however, many very ancient cult sites: the altars of Zeus Hypatos (Supreme), Poseidon and Erechtheus, the hero Boutes (Erechtheus' brother) and of the god Hephaestus, as well as the rock bearing the mark of Poseidon's trident, from whence gushed the salt water that the god offered to the city. Another tradition holds that this mark on the rock was from Zeus' thunderbolt when he killed Erechtheus. In order for the point where the thunderbolt struck to be visible, a section of the roof was left open. The 'Erechthian Sea' was located under

Reconstruction of the west side of the Erechtheion. To the right can be seen the porch of the Korai and to the left the luxurious propylon gate, which had six columns arranged in a Π, a roof with painted marble panels and an entrance with a sculpted doorway. The continuous frieze with its enigmatic subject (perhaps scenes inspired by the cults housed in the Erechtheion) can also be seen. Inside the building, in front of the goddess's statue, burnt a gold lamp, the work of the famous 5th-century sculptor Callimachus, who, according to Pausanias, would fill it with oil only once annually, and this was enough to keep the flame going for a year, night and day. Upon it there was a tall bronze phoenix to funnel the smoke away.

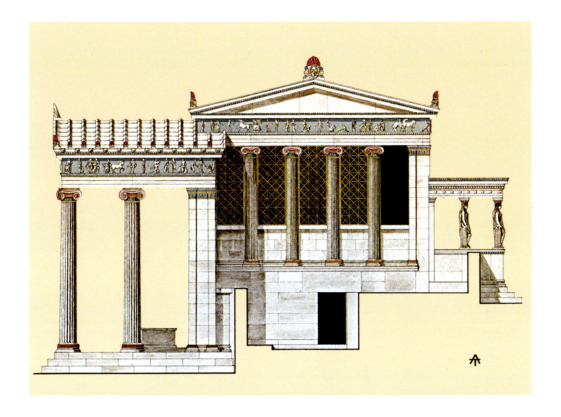

The Erechtheion from the southwest in a 19th-century drawing. The first centuries of the temple's life were peaceful, although it caught fire in the 1st century BC, perhaps during Sulla's destruction of the city (86 BC). It was repaired during the reign of the emperor Augustus and converted into a church during the Early Christian period, with extensive alterations to its interior. It also suffered great destruction from a Turkish canon during the 1821 revolution. The earliest restoration work on the monument, to the porch of the Korai, was done in the mid-19th century.

the marble floor, the cistern of seawater from where, Pausanias writes, waves could be heard when the south wind was blowing. The sacred 'household snake', a creature associated with both Erechtheus and Athens, lived in the Erechtheion.

The construction of the Erechtheion dates to 421-409 BC. Its architect remains unknown, although some scholars believe it may have been Mnesikles. Irrespective of who he was, the architect of the Erechtheion had to incorporate all these differing cult elements in one space, as well as to take into account the changes in ground level. The result was one of the most unusual religious buildings of antiquity. The Erechtheion is comprised of a main building divided into two sections (the east section was dedicated to the cult of Athena Polias and the west to Poseidon/Erechtheus) to which were added two lateral structures, the north porch and the porch of the Korai. It was built on four different levels and had three different roofs, a luxury propylon gate with painted marble panels, and Ionic columns of three different sizes. Its original frieze of grey Eleusinian stone was decorated with figures in the round made from Pentelic marble and, following an old Ionian custom, statues of Korai were used as columns. Years after the temple was built the Korai of the Erechtheion began to be called the

Caryatids. The most convincing explanation for this new name is that it was derived from the girls of the town of Karyai in Laconia, who danced a famous dance in honour of the goddess Artemis.

The 'old temple'

The excavations of 1885 brought to light, to the south of the Erechtheion, the foundations of a large peripteral temple, belonging to the 'old temple'. We know of the existence of this temple from the ancient sources, but what we do not know is precisely when it was built. In the past, it had been believed that the temple was built in 570 BC and renovated in around 525 BC by the sons of the tyrant Peisistratus. Another view, however, based on the study of the architectural details, is that the temple and the sculptural marble decoration were created in the last decade of the 6th century BC, making the temple a product of the young Athenian democracy.

The 'old temple' was dedicated to the peaceful Athena Polias, the protector of the city, and housed the 'heaven-sent' wooden cult statue of the goddess until 406 BC, when this venerable effigy was trans-

The Caryatids that one sees on the south porch of the Erechtheion today are faithful copies of the six beautiful originals. In contrast with the archaic sculptures that were discovered during the 19th-century excavations, the Caryatids were always visible on the Acropolis. Legend has it that after Lord Elgin removed one of the Caryatids the Athenians could hear her sisters mourning her at night.

The Erechtheion, the 'house of Erechtheus'. Myth holds that the Athenians once fought with the Eleusinians whose king, Eumolpos, was the son of Poseidon. The Athenians won and their king, Erechtheus, killed Eumolpos. Poseidon was outraged and asked his brother Zeus to take revenge. Zeus shot down one of his lightening bolts, cutting the thread of Erechtheus's life.

ferred to the newly-built Erechtheion. The 'old temple', which replaced an earlier Geometric temple to Athena, was Doric with 6 x 12 columns and pediments adorned with figures in the round made of Parian marble. One pediment featured the Gigantomachy (battle between gods and Giants), whilst only fragments of a group with a lion tearing a bull to pieces survive from the other pediment. Their creation has been attributed to either Antenor or Endoios, famous sculptors of the day. After the Persian raid of the Acropolis in 480 BC the 'old temple' was temporarily repaired, only to be destroyed once more during a fire in 406 BC. Some believe that it was again repaired and remained in use until at least the mid-4th century BC, although others believe that it was never again repaired.

The Pandroseion

A small door in the west wall of the Erechtheion led to the sanctuary of Pandrosos, daughter of the mythical king Kekrops. Here stood the altar of Zeus Herekios already since the Mycenaean period, the tomb of Kekrops, a part of which extended under the porch of the

Karyatids, and the olive tree that Athena had granted to the city. Tradition holds that when the Persians set fire to the sanctuary in 480 BC, the following day a shoot one cubit (46 cm) high sprouted from the charred trunk. A new olive tree was planted in the early 20th century approximately on the spot of the ancient one.

The Arrhephorion

The 5th-century BC building whose foundations are to be found near the wall to the northwest of the Erechtheion has been identified with the Arrhephorion, the house of the Arrhephorai. The Arrhephorai were girls aged between 7 and 11, from the leading families of Athens, who lived for a brief period in the sanctuary of Athena. They were thus named because they carried the *arrheta*, i.e. the 'unspeakable objects', during the festival of the Arrhephoria, in the month of Skirophorion (approximately mid-June to mid-July). As we are informed by Pausanias, on the night of the mystery ritual they would take the sacred objects, covered so that they could not see them, and go down to the north slope of the Acropolis through a secret passage that led into the adjacent sanctuary of Aphrodite and Eros. Here a member of the priesthood would receive the sacred objects and give the Arrhephorai some other objects, also carefully covered, which they would then take back up to the Acropolis in the same way, where they would hand them over to the priestess of Athena. With the taking of the new holy objects to the Acropolis, the service of the Arrhephorai ended and they returned to their homes, to be replaced by other girls. The Arrhephorai also participated in the weaving of the new *peplos* cloak for the cult statue of Athena, which was taken to the Acropolis by the Panathenaic procession. The young girls who lived in this building would enjoy themselves by playing with a small ball in a small yard known as the '*sphairistra* (ball court) of the Arrhephorai'.

Reconstruction of the facade of the sanctuary of Artemis Brauronia (G.P. Stevens). The goddess's ancient xoanon (wooden cult statue), similar to that at Brauron, would have been housed within the sanctuary, perhaps in one of the closed side wings of the stoa. At Brauron, as the 2nd-century AD traveller Pausanias noted, there was also a new cult statue of Artemis, a work of the famous sculptor Praxiteles (mid-4th century BC). As we learn from the inscriptions, the women who sought the goddess's help dressed her statue in clothes.

Artemis, daughter of Zeus and sister of Apollo the god of light, was the protector of nature, wild animals, childbirth and newborns. She was also closely connected with Iphigenia, daughter of king Agamemnon, who was to be sacrificed at the goddess's alter in Aulis, so that the sails of the Greek ships could spread and set sail for Troy. The goddess saved the girl at the last moment, however, and led her to the land of the Taurians. On her return to Greece, Iphigenia brought the cult of Artemis to Brauron. In this representation, the goddess Artemis spreads her arms out tenderly to a swan. White-ground lekythos, ca 490 BC. St Petersburg, Hermitage.

The sanctuary of Artemis Brauronia

The foundations of a sanctuary dedicated to Artemis Brauronia, protector of women in pregnancy and childbirth, have been found to the southeast of the Propylaia. It is believed that the Brauroneion on the Acropolis functioned as an annex of her great sanctuary at Brauron, on the eastern coasts of Attica. Here, tradition holds, Iphigenia, daughter of the mythical king Agamemnon, set up the wooden cult statue of the goddess which she had brought with her from the Taurus Peninsula. Worship of Artemis on the Acropolis was established in the mid-6th century BC and is attributed to the tyrant Peisistratus, who hailed from the region of Mesogaia.

From the few traces of the Brauroneion that have survived, we know that the main section of the sanctuary was comprised of a Π-shaped Doric stoa, the back of which rested against the south wall of the Acropolis. The sanctuary was bordered by an enclosure wall on its north side, the entrance being in the northeast corner. In the 5th century BC a stairwell with seven steps, still visible today, was constructed here, and some believe that there was perhaps also a small temple within the precinct.

The Chalkotheke

The foundations of a long, narrow building of the mid-5th century BC have been found adjacent to the Brauroneion, on its east side. In the 4th century BC a stoa with 20 columns was added to its facade. The building has been identified with the Chalkotheke, known from inscriptions, where bronze items were stored, such as weapons, statuettes and hydrias, offerings by the faithful to the goddess Athena.

The sanctuary of Pandion

A sanctuary in honour of Pandion, the mythical king of Athens, was established to the east of the Parthenon, where the building of the old Acropolis Museum is to be found today. The sanctuary is comprised of a large rectangular precinct, divided into two sections.

The temple of Rome and Augustus

To the east of the Parthenon or, from another point of view, to the east of the Erechtheion, there stood a small temple which the Athenians had dedicated to the goddess Rome and the emperor Augustus. Built in the Ionic order, this was a circular, monopteros (without a wall behind its colonnade) building with a conical roof. The surviving votive inscription on the epistyle helps us to date it to after 27 BC, as it was after this date that Octavian, nephew and adopted son of Julius Caesar, took the title Augustus and began to rule Rome as emperor.

The sanctuary of Zeus Polieus

The sanctuary of Zeus Polieus, of which there are only scant traces, is located close to the northeast corner of the Parthenon. In its original form the sanctuary included a rectangular precinct, a small temple, an altar table and a pit for sacrificial ashes hewn into the rock. Here, during the Athenian Diipolia festival, an ox was sacrificed each year on the 14th day of the month of Skirophorion (late June), as described by Pausanias. Barley mixed with wheat was scattered over the god's altar. When the ox to be sacrificed approached and started eating the grains, he was killed by one of the priests known as the *bouphonos* (ox-killer), who then dashed off and disappeared. The Athenians would then put the murder weapon, an axe, on trial. This strange custom is associated, according to modern interpretations, with the transition of the

An impressive marble dog, produced in around 520 BC. Along with a second similar statue, fragments of which survive, it adorned the entrance to the sanctuary of Artemis Brauronia. This wonderful depiction of a skinny dog, which looks as though it is about to pounce on its prey, is attributed to the creator of the Rampin horseman. Athens, Acropolis Museum, Level I, Archaic Gallery, Acr. 143.

cult from its prehistoric phase, when grains were offered to the gods, to the later phase when bloody sacrifices were demanded. Pausanias saw two sculptures in the sanctuary, an older and a newer one, a work of the sculptor Leochares (*ca* 330 BC).

The altar of Athena

Some cuttings in the rock in front of the sanctuary of Zeus Polieus and to the west have identified the location of the very ancient altar of Athena. This was the main, great altar to the goddess and for centuries served all the temples that were built on the Acropolis rock.

The votives

The appearance of the Acropolis in antiquity was, of course, completely different from that of today. For a start, the Rock was enclosed by a high wall, creating for pilgrims a sense of isolation from the external environment. High retaining walls also created different levels, so that each building would stand autonomously within its own private space. A large, almost square quad extended in front of the Propylaia. Finally, in each corner of the sanctuary there stood wonderful bronze and marble statues, dedicated by the faithful to the goddess Athena (the Greek word for statue, *agalma*, derives from the word *agallomai*, to be very happy, joyous; through their votives the faithful offered joy to the god or goddess). Very few traces of statues set up after the Persian destruction of the Acropolis have survived. Their former presence is confirmed only by some carvings in the rock and the works of Pausanias and other ancient authors.

In the mid-5th century BC the Athenian colonists on Lemnos set up a bronze statue of the goddess Athena by Phidias on the Acropolis. The ancient sources praised the statue's beauty. Roman copy of the Lemnian Athena. Head: Bologna, Museo Civico, Body: Dresden, Staatliche Kunstsammlungen Skulpturensammlung (where the statute illustrated is housed, with a plaster cast head).

The most impressive of all was undoubtedly the colossal bronze statue of Athena Promachos, which stood resplendent opposite the Propylaia. This was one of the early works of Phidias, which the Athenians commissioned with the booty from Kimon's victory over the Persians at the River Eurymedon (467 BC). In the same area, although unknown at which point exactly, a second work of Phidias, the statue of Lemnian Athena, which had been dedicated by Athenian *cleruchs* of Lemnos (Athenian citizens who had been allotted a parcel of land in ally or vassal cities) in the mid-5th century BC. Near the east side of the Propylaia there was also a bronze statue of Athena Hygeia (Health), a work of the sculptor Pyrrhus. It is believed that this statue was set up here after the plague that decimated the inhabitants of the city at the beginning of the Peloponnesian War (429-427 BC). A little further down, in the west section of the Brauroneion, a base was discovered which is believed to be that of the huge bronze Trojan horse by the sculptor Strongylion (late 5th c. BC).

Yet another votive mentioned by Pausanias, a statue of the goddess Gaia 'who invokes Zeus to send rain', was located in the middle of the north colonnade of the Parthenon, where the inscription 'of fruit-bearing Gaia, according to an oracle' is inscribed in the rock. This sculpture was dedicated by the Athenians in around AD 100 after a period of drought. Further to the east stood the statues of the general Conon and his son Timoethos, who contributed to the revival of Athenian leadership after the end of the Peloponnesian War (404 BC). Somewhere nearby there was a statue of Procne, daughter of

According to the myth, Procne, the daughter of the Athenian king Pandion, discovered that her husband Tereus had raped her sister Philomela and had cut out her tongue so that she could not tell of this unholy act. Procne killed their son Itys and fed him to Tereus. Once Tereus realised he started to persecute the two sisters. The gods then transformed Procne into a nightingale who cried for her son by cooing 'itys, itys', Philomela into a swallow and Tereus into a hoopoe. This group of Procne and Itys is identified as the piece that Pausanias saw on the Acropolis and which he believed to be a votive from Alkamenes, student of Phidias. 430 BC. Athens, Acropolis Museum, Level I, North section, Acr. 1358.

Pandion, today housed in the Acropolis Museum. Of the remaining sculptures that once adorned the Acropolis, mention should be made of the bust of Pericles, who had inspired the finest buildings on the Sacred Rock. This bust had been executed by Kresilas, a pupil of Phidias. In addition to the sculptures, the wealth of the sanctuary was increased by a variety of other votives, such as vessels and utensils or reliefs and statuettes of marble, bronze and terracotta.

The wall

A refuge for the inhabitants of the region during the prehistoric period, the Acropolis was surrounded in the 13th century BC by a wall which, as scholars believe, was maintained with a few modifications and reinforcements until 480 BC, when it suffered great damage under the Persians. After the end of the Persian Wars, the fortifications of the Acropolis were restored with the construction of the north wall, the so-called Themistoklean. In this they used pieces of building material, visible even today, which had come from the ruined sacred structures of the Acropolis.

The south wall, known as the Kimonian, was built in the years of the Athenian general Kimon after his victory against the Persians at the River Eurymedon (467 BC). It was built using isodomic masonry, although most of the wall was covered during the repairs in the medieval and modern periods.

The old Acropolis Museum

The old Acropolis Museum was built in 1865, on designs by the architect P. Kalkos, within a hollow in the rock, so as not to alter the image of the archaeological site. It welcomed its visitors for almost 150 years, showing them the wonderful works of the ancient Athenians. This historic Museum passed the baton on to the new Acropolis Museum in 2009 without, however, being decommissioned. It will soon open as a Museum once more, presenting the history of the Sacred Rock, copies of works by foreign travellers who visited the Acropolis (15th-19th centuries), the history of earlier excavations, as well as the history of the old and contemporary restoration work on the monuments.

THE SOUTH SLOPE OF THE ACROPOLIS

From the 5th century BC the south slope of the Acropolis was one of the most important centres of the religious and cultural life of Athens. The Athenians would gather at the Odeion of Pericles and later at that of Herodes Atticus to follow musical contests, at the sanctuary of the Nymph they would bring their offerings so that their marriages would succeed, and to the sanctuary of Asclepius went all those who suffered from a trauma or an illness to restore their hopes. A little further down, at the theatre of Dionysus, the sufferings of Oedipus, Medeia, Orestes, the heroes of ancient Greek drama, were brought to life in front of their eyes.

After the end of the ancient world the appearance of the south slope changed greatly. During the 5th-6th century AD and in the area of the Asclepeion an Early Christian basilica was built, mainly using ancient building material, dedicated to the doctor saints of Christianity, the Agioi Anargyroi. A second Early Christian basilica was founded in the east passageway of the theatre of Dionysus. Later, during the 11th and 12th centuries AD, the church of Saint George the Alexandrian was built over the now ruined east basilica. This church fell victim to hostilities during the Greek War of Independence, and its site is today occupied by a small 19th-century church. The arrival of the Frank conquerors in the first half of the 13th century brought other changes to Athens, including the construction of a new wall around the foot of the Acropolis, called the Rizokastro. Its south section, from the Herodeion to the Theatre of Dionysus, known as the bastion of Serpentze, survived until the first period of Ottoman rule (1456-1687). During these years, the 15th or 16th century, it appears that the south slope, which had been deserted during the Frankish period, started to be inhabited again. Another wall, although irregular, was built in 1778, under the *voivoide* (governor) Hatzi-Ali Haseki, as protection from Albanian raids. Remains of Haseki's wall, which surrounded the city, as well as sections not built upon, are still preserved around the Acropolis. As for the ancient monuments, as we can see in the drawings made by travellers during the Ottoman period and the 19th century, they were almost all covered over by mounds of earth. The creation of the modern Greek state after the 1821 revolution, however, ushered in the last phase of history for the south slope: the formation of an impressive archaeological site, where research and conservation and rehabilitation works continue.

The Acropolis rock from the southwest, with the Odeion of Herodes Atticus and the other buildings of the south slope at its foot. The morphology of the terrain on the south slope and the presence of drinkable water were

from very early on a draw for the inhabitants of the region. They thus built
their houses here and established important sanctuaries and theatres,
cultivating the city's cultural life.

The monumental, inscribed cylindrical altar of Dionysus (NK 292) exhibited in the store near the entrance to the South Slope archaeological site. Its surface is decorated with relief Satyr masks, medallions and tendrils of ivy leaves, acanthus and fruits (ivy was one of the symbols of Dionysus whilst the goat-like Satyrs were members of his escort). 2nd century BC.

Exhibits store

Sculptures from the Theatre of Dionysus and finds from the wider area of the god's sanctuary are exhibited in a covered exhibits stores near the entrance to the archaeological site, on the right. Here one can see, amongst other items, two rather damaged marble sculptures of women from the Theatre, perhaps personifications of Tragedy and Comedy (1st c. AD). Moreover, the impressive lower section of a colossal statue of perhaps a female divinity, where we can see a paddle or rudder and relief waves, and another colossal statue of a naked Old Silenus, from the *skene* of the Theatre of Dionysus (1st-2nd c.

Statue of Old Silenus (NK 2295), dating to the 1st or 2nd century AD, inside the exhibits store located near the entrance of the archaeological site. The zoo-morphic Old Silenus, the oldest of the Silens, was also part of the god Dionysus's escort and according to one myth he was his teacher. This impressive figure adorned, along with other similar ones, the Roman stage of the Theatre of Dionysus.

AD). This latter may have stood in the pose of Atlas, the mythical Titan who bore the weight of the heavens on his shoulders or, according to another version, the heavens and the earth together. Our attention is drawn to the monumental, inscribed cylindrical altar of Dionysus (2nd c. BC) and the inscribed and unfluted column in honour of Ariobarzanes II, king of Cappadocia and funder of the renovation of the Odeion of Pericles (63/2 - 52/1 BC). Also, the large inscribed stele bearing two decrees granting privileges to the Athenian 'artists of Dionysus', i.e. those who put on the dramatic productions (278/7 and 130/29 BC), and a votive pedestal with an inscription honouring the archon Gaius Julius Antiochus Epiphanes Philopappus and mentioning

Aeschylus (525-456 BC) first appeared on the Athenian scene in around 500 BC. To him are attributed innovations such as the addition of a second actor, which significantly spurred the development of drama. He wrote around ninety works, of which only seven survive complete. Characteristic of the sprit of the era is the fact that, in keeping with his wishes, his funerary epigram mentioned only his participation at the battle of Marathon. Roman copy of a 4th-century BC bust of Aeschylus. Naples, Museo Archeologico Nazionale.

the contributors to the production performed at the Dionysia (AD 75/6 - 87/8). We should note that the mausoleum on the hill south-west of the Acropolis, in antiquity known as Mouseion Hill, is that of Philopappus, and, thanks to his tomb, the hill is today known as Philopappus Hill.

The ancient roads

One of the best-known roads of ancient Athens was the *Peripatos*, which circled the Acropolis rock and which many Athenians chose for their summer evening walks. We know of its name and total length (5 stadia and 18 feet, i.e. 1,100 metres) from a 4th-century BC inscription carved into the rock of the north slope. The Peripatos was a central road from which branched off footpaths and stairs leading to the sanctuaries on the slopes and to the secondary entrances to the Acropolis. Main roads, which were either associated with ritual events or part of the ancient city's road network, also terminated here. One of the most central roads to be encountered on the Peripatos – the most important road in ancient Athens, to be precise – was the Panathenaic Way, the road taken by the sacred procession during the great feast. The Panathenaic Way started at the Dipylon, the main gate to the city, and passed through the ancient Agora and western part of the north slope, to end at the Propylaia. The Peripatos also intersected another road with an interesting history, the Street of the Tripods, which began at the Prytaneion in the ancient Agora and reached as far as the Theatre of Dionysus. Along its length the *choregoi* (sponsors) of the plays that had won prizes would set up the tripods that the *deme* of Athens had offered them as votives. These tripods, most of which were bronze and more rarely gilded or silver-plated, were set up upon bases, some simple others more elaborate, and also in small temple-like buildings, some of which still survive today.

Three of the ancient roads discovered during archaeological excavations meet outside the southeast corner of the sanctuary of Dionysus, very close to the entrance to the archaeological site of the south slope. The remains of a small *roadside poros temple* of the 5th century BC, dedicated to an unknown deity, perhaps Hermes or Hecate, a goddess associated with crossroads, were uncovered here. The remains of a Christian monument are visible to the south of the enclosure wall and the small roadside temple: a single-aisled *basilica* dedicated to *Saint Paraskevi* built in three phases from the late Byzantine period to the 19th century.

The sanctuary of Dionysus Eleuthereus

The sanctuary of Dionysus on the south slope of the Acropolis was founded in the 6th century BC, in the years of the tyrant Peisistratus. It was called the sanctuary of Dionysus Eleuthereus because the god's cult had been introduced from the originally Boeotian and subsequently Attic *deme* of Eleutherai. A Doric temple was built at this time, and a circular area developed a little to the north for the performance of cult rituals in honour of Dionysus. This formed the core of the subsequent theatre. Later, during the second half of the 4th century BC, the sanctuary acquired a new temple to the south of the earlier one, which was not, however, abandoned. Most scholars believe that the new temple was also Doric and that it housed the chryselephantine statue of the god by the celebrated sculptor Alkamenes. Only a few traces survive of the two temples today, as is also the case with the altar located to the southeast of the later temple and which appears to have been constructed at the same time or shortly after it. Excavations have, however, revealed the remains of a stoa which must have been built during the time of the renovation of the sanctuary and the theatre by the Athenian orator Lycurgus (*ca* 330 BC). This stoa defined the sanctuary's boundary in the north, whereas there was an enclosure wall on the other three sides and a propylon gate in the east.

Aristophanes (ca 445-386 BC), the leading comic playwright of antiquity, confronted and bravely satirised his era from the perspective of the average Athenian. In this way his comedies, in addition to their great artistic value, give us the opportunity to get to know the lives and thoughts of ordinary people during the difficult years of the Peloponnesian War. Roman copy of a 4th-century BC bust of Aristophanes. Paris, Musée du Louvre.

The Theatre of Dionysus Eleuthereus

The Theatre of Dionysus is integrally connected to one of the most brilliant creations of the ancient Greeks: drama, the ancestor of the modern theatre. There has been much debate on the birth and development of ancient Greek drama. The prevailing view holds that its roots lie in the dithyramb, the improvised song that the faithful sang as they danced in honour of the god Dionysus, god of vegetation, wine and intoxication. Gradually, with the introduction of new elements, the dithyramb developed into the first complete theatrical expression of the western world, ancient Greek drama. All three forms of ancient drama – tragedy, satyr and comedy – were perfected in the Athens of the 5th century BC. The works of the three great tragic poets of the era – Aeschylus, Sophocles and Euripides as well as of the comic poet Aristophanes, remain even until today living monuments of an unequalled art form.

The theatre in ancient Athens was completely different to that of today: it was a part of the religious events and took the form of a

In the ancient period the actors, always men, appeared in front of the audience dressed in impressive costumes and masks which covered their whole head. By changing their costumes and masks they could act the various male and female, mythical and real characters of the play.
Detail from the Pronomos Vase: two actors, in their masks and costumes, after the end of a performance. Late 5th century BC. Naples, Museo Archeologico Nazionale.

competition. During the 5th and a large part of the 4th century BC the dramatic contests were primarily held during the Great or City Dionysia, the splendid annual festival in honour of Dionysus, which took place during the month of Elaphebolion (late March-early April). Three tragic and five (later three) comic playwrights would be selected to take part in these contests and present their plays to the public, one after another, from sunrise to sunset over the duration of specific days. Ancient drama, whether tragedy, satyr plays or comedy, had two basic elements: first, monologues and dialogues between the actors and, secondly, songs that were sung by a group of people, the chorus, accompanied by rhythmic movements. At the end of all the performances a ten-member committee would announce the winner.

For the ancient Athenians, the dramatic contests were one of the city's finest institutions, an inexhaustible source of cultural creativity. For this reason they were followed by all, rich and poor, as from very early on the city had undertaken to provide poor citizens with the price of the ticket. The city also selected the *choregoi* (sponsors), the wealthy Athenians who would fund part of the expenses for each performance.

The theatre of Dionysus, this exceptionally important monument of the south slope, is located to the north of the sanctuary. As with all ancient theatres, it is comprised of three sections: the *orchestra* (from *orchoumai* = to dance, a circular platform upon which the action took place), the *skene* (a long, narrow building in which the actors changed clothes and which was usually used as scenery) and the *cavea* or *koilon* (an amphitheatre-shaped hollow in the slope with seats for the audience). It did not, however, always have the form in which it survives today. Initially, in the 6th century BC, all that existed here was the *orchestra*, the circular space of trodden earth specially designed for the rituals of the cult of Dionysus, which the faithful observed seated on the slopes of the hill. Wooden seats were later placed here. In the 5th century BC, the period of the great ancient playwrights, the *cavea* or *koilon*, where the audience was seated, was expanded, although we are not certain of its precise form. It is, however, certain that the wooden seats were replaced by stone ones and steps were built for the first time, dividing the *cavea* into rows. The theatre acquired a monumental form in the time of Lycurgus, around 330 BC, when the *cavea* was expanded to the foot of the rock, thus incorporating a section of the Peripatos walk and turning it into a *diazoma*, or walkway (the section of the *cavea* above the *diazoma* is known as the Epitheatron). It has been calculated that during this phase the theatre seated an audience of 15-16,000, who would be sitting, from now on, on stone seats. The first row of seats, the so-called presidency, was comprised of 67 marble thrones, true works of art, each with the

View of the theatre of Dionysus. The building that one can see today dates mostly to the years of the Athenian archon and orator Lycurgus (second half of the 4th century BC), the period during which the permanent seats were made using Piraeus limestone (quarried at the Piraeus coast). In the Roman period, due to the extension of the skene, the circular orchestra was converted into a semicircle and laid with marble slabs. The upright marble slabs, which form a parapet around the orchestra, were obviously used so as to fill the orchestra with water for the performance of naval battle scenes, a popular show in Roman times.

name of the official for which it was intended carved onto it. The throne of the priest of Dionysus Eleuthereus in the centre was the most distinguished. During this period, in addition to the seats, the *skene* was also rebuilt in stone, now a rectangular building with two protruding wings at the edges, the *paraskenia*. The *skene* was the part of the Theatre the form of which changed the most over the centuries. In the 2nd or 1st century BC a second floor was built (with the

Figures from the relief slabs that adorn the Bema of Phaedrus in the theatre of Dionysus. The skene of this very ancient theatre underwent many changes, especially from the Roman period onwards. It was damaged during Sulla's invasion in 86 BC, although it was repaired, possibly by Ariobarzanes II, king of Cappadocia. In the first century AD, during the reign of Nero, it took on an intensely monumental character, whilst the so-called Bema of Phaedrus was later created in front of it.

development of theatrical forms the role of the chorus declined and the lead actors became the protagonists, with the action shifting from the *orchestra* to the *skene*). Later, under the emperor Nero (mid 1st century AD) a new luxury *skene* was constructed, with impressive dimensions. In the mid 2nd or the 3rd century AD a tall stage was built in front of the *skene*. In the early 5th century AD the notable Phaedrus, amongst other changes, incorporated relief plaques from an earlier building, with subjects from the life of Dionysus (Bema of Phaedrus) into the stage.

The Theatre of Dionysus Eleuthereus was abandoned after the end of antiquity and was gradually covered by earth during the medieval period. It was brought to light again by excavations conducted between 1862 and 1895. The most recent work to take place here was the clearing of the *cavea* from 1998 to 2004, followed by conservation and renovation work.

The marble throne in the first row of seats in the theatre of Dionysus, which was reserved for the members of the Athenian priesthood. Inscriptions on each throne preserve the title of the individual for whom the throne was reserved. In the centre, as one might expect, was the throne of the priest of Dionysus Eleuthereus.

The Odeion of Pericles

To the east of the Theatre of Dionysus there formerly stood a huge, square building with internal colonnades and a pyramid-shaped roof in imitation, so the tradition goes, of the tent of the Persian king Xerxes.

This was the odeion that was constructed in the time of Pericles, the first roofed building in Athens to be used for the musical contests of the Panathenaia and other musical events. The Odeion of Pericles was burnt down in 86 BC during the siege of Athens by the Roman general Sulla by the defenders of the building themselves, so that its plentiful wood would not fall in the hands of the Romans. A little later it was rebuilt by the king of Cappadocia Ariobarzanes and continued to be in use until razed to the ground by the Herulians (AD 267).

The choregic monument of Thrasyllus

A small cave can be seen above the Theatre of Dionysus where the choregic monument of Thrasyllus was built in 320/319 BC. According to scholars the monument consists of a constructed marble facade in front of the natural cave, with two marble pillars and a pillar flanked by antae, a Doric architrave and an Ionic frieze decorated with an ivy wreath in the centre. On each side there were olive wreaths. Above the geison stood the choregic tripod. A number of decades later, in 271/270 BC, Thrasykles the son of Thrasyllus had two victories as a *choregos* and set up another two tripods. It later became a place of worship, it is believed from the early Christian period, whilst in the 17th century, as we learn from foreign travellers, it was developed into an idiosyncratic, two-part church known as the Panagia Chrysospilio-tissa. Travellers' drawings show another modification, dating to the Roman period, when the tripod of Thrasyllus was replaced by a marble statue of Dionysus. In 1802 this statue fell into the hands of Lord Elgin, and is thus today exhibited in the British Museum. Despite the renovations, the monument of Thrasyllus was preserved almost intact until the siege of the Acropolis by the Turks in 1827. A little later, in the mid-19th century, the Athens Archaeological Society announced that it intended to restore the monument but, however, unbelievable it may sound, the scattered building material was pillaged and used to restore the Byzantine church of the Saviour of Nikodemos (Russian church), in Filellinon Street. Modern reconstruction work on the monument of Thrasyllus, guided by the drawings of the British architects Nicholas Stuart and James Revett who visited Athens in 1751-3, started in 2002.

A little higher up from the monument of Thrasyllus there survive two impressive columns dating to the Roman period, crowned by a further two choregic tripods.

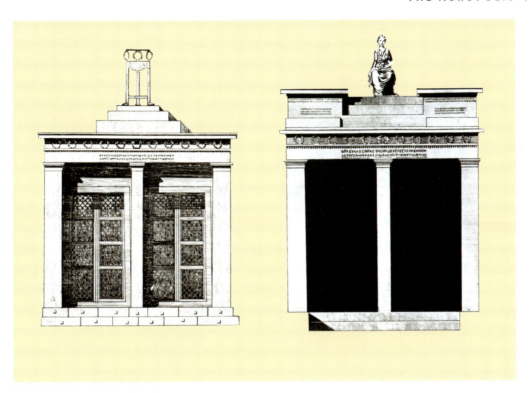

The choregic monument of Nikias

The remains of the foundations of the choregic monument set up by Nikias, son of Nikodemos, were discovered to the west of the road going up past the sanctuary of Dionysus. This was a temple-shaped building of Pentelic marble with six columns on the facade, built for Nikias' choregic victory in the dramatic contests of 320/319 BC. The choregic monument of Nikias was dismantled in AD 237 and most of its material used in the construction of the Beulé Gate, to the west of the Propylaia.

The Stoa of Eumenes

To the northwest of the choregic monument of Nikias a huge stoa was built in around 160 BC, the expenses being paid for by the Pergamene king Eumenes II (197-159 BC). The Athenians would gather here during the intervals of theatrical performances or to discuss affairs, when the weather prevented them from remaining outdoors.

In order to construct the stoa the area to the south of the Asclepeion terrace and the Peripatos was dug up to create a huge artificial

The choregic monument of Thrasyllus during the first phase of its history, left, and, right, as it was rendered by the British architects Stuart and Revett in the mid-18th century. The inscription stating that the 'Dekelian Thrsasyllus son of Thrasyllus' won a choregic victory during the archonship of Neaichmos can be seen in both drawings. Pausanias, who visited the monument in the 2nd century AD, informs us that there was an image of Apollo and Artemis killing the children of Niobe inside the cave. Myth holds that Niobe, queen of Thebes, had insulted their mother Leto, claiming that she was much happier than her because she had many children and Leto only two.

View of the remains of the giant stoa that the king of Pergamon, Eumenes II, bestowed upon the Athenians in around 160 BC. Experts believe that a type of island marble was used in its construction, which can be found in most buildings at Pergamon but nowhere else in Athens. It is believed that a large part of its architectural pieces were constructed in Pergamon and then transported here ready-made.

plateau. A strong retaining wall was constructed to support the earth fill of the Peripatos, reinforced with struts unified by an arcade. Along the length of this wall a two-floor stoa of approximately 163 metres in length and 17 metres in width was constructed, with 64 Doric columns on the facade of the ground floor and an Ionic colonnade of 32 columns in its interior. Correspondingly, the external colonnade on the upper floor was comprised of Ionic half columns, while on the interior there was a colonnade with Pergamene capitals. The facade had many similarities with the stoa of Attalus in the ancient Agora of Athens, the donor of which was Eumenes' brother Attalus II.

The stoa of Eumenes remained in use until the 3rd century AD, when it was used as building material in the construction of the late Roman wall. Much later, in the mid-13th century AD, its north retaining wall was incorporated into the Rizokastro, the wall built around the foot of the Acropolis. Today, this once grand stoa is now an object of study and sections of it are being restored.

The Asclepeion

The sanctuary of Asclepius, the most important on the South Slope after that of Dionysus, is a space where people could worship the

In recent years work has been carried out on the stoa of Eumenes to arrange its wealth of fragmentary material as well as to identify and reassemble its architectural pieces. As part of the instructive reconstruction of sections of the building, the column in the photograph has been set up. It originally came from the internal colonnade of the monument's roof and has a Pergamene capital.

The restored section of the Doric stoa of Asclepius. Repairs to the building were carried out in the 1st century BC, perhaps before Sulla's raid, and it was also rebuilt in the 2nd or 4th century AD.

healing god and which also functioned as a treatment centre. The finest sanctuary to Asclepius and at the same time the finest treatment centre in the whole ancient Greek and Roman world was located at Epidaurus in the Peloponnese. There were also Asclepeia at dozens of other places throughout the Mediterranean, where people would go for treatment of the illnesses that ailed them. At first, treatment depended entirely on the god, although later medical science also contributed to successful outcomes.

As we know from the inscribed double-sided relief housed in the Acropolis Museum, the sanctuary of Asclepius on the South Slope was founded by an Athenian citizen, Telemachus, in 420/419 BC. The sanctuary occupied two terraces in the east and west, to the west of the *cavea* of the Theatre of Dionysus and to the north of the Peripatos. A two-floor *Doric stoa* was built on the east terrace in 300/299 BC, which contained in its east section the *Sacred Fountain*, a small cave with a spring (water was a primary element of the god's cult). The *Sacred Pit* was discovered on the west edge, a well dating to the 5th century BC where the Heroa were held, a festival with sacrifices to chthonian gods and heroes. Specialists believe that this stoa functioned as an *Engoimeterion*, a place, that is, where patients slept in the hope that they would be healed through miraculous dreams. In front of this stoa were the *altar* and *temple* of the god, of which foundations dating to the early Roman period survive. A second, smaller *stoa* was built further south in the Roman period. The remnants of the sanctuary's *propylon* gate were discovered next to it, in the west, although these are not visible today. A third *stoa* now dominated over the second terrace, which researchers believe was built prior to the temple and later incorporated into the sanctuary with the addition of an Ionic colonnade to its facade. This Ionic stoa, as it is called, had four square rooms furnished with couches at the back and was used as lodgings and a 'banqueting hall' for the priests or visitors to the Asclepeion.

Very near to the Ionic stoa of Asclepius there was a *sanctuary* dedicated to the *Nymphs*, *Hermes* and the goat-legged god *Pan*, as well as an archaic *fountain,* dating to around 520 BC. In the Byzantine period a *well* was constructed on its west wing, which when it overflowed would funnel the water to another larger *well* further south (the latter was conserved and used as a store for findings from the site). The foundations of two *temples* were discovered in very fragmentary condition near the ancient fountain, one tentatively attributed to *Themis*, the goddess of justice, and the other to *Isis*, an Egyptian goddess whose cult was imported into Greece.

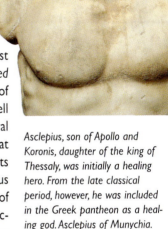

Asclepius, son of Apollo and Koronis, daughter of the king of Thessaly, was initially a healing hero. From the late classical period, however, he was included in the Greek pantheon as a healing god. Asclepius of Munychia. 2nd century BC. Athens, National Archaeological Museum.

The Asclepeion, the sanctuary of the god of medicine Asclepius, from above. Experts believe that the temple of Asclepius was a simple cella within which the god's statue was housed. Behind the temple was the so-called Doric stoa, which is believed to have been used as an abaton or as an engoimeterion. This stoa had two floors with an internal Doric colonnade on both floors.

Exhibits store

Inscribed finds from the sanctuary have been collected in the exhibits store the visitor will come to after the Asclepeion, including poros and marble votive stelai, marble herms with honorary inscriptions and marble pediments with honorary inscriptions. Two marble altars have been placed in the centre of the store, one dedicated to Herakles (3rd-2nd century BC) and the other to Hermes, Aphrodite, Pan, the Nymphs and Isis (1st century BC).

The Chalkourgeion

The contemporary stone wall to the west of the exhibits store encloses the remains of a Chalkourgeion, or bronze-casting installation. The best preserved of its sections is the southeast, possibly from the 5th century BC, which includes a poros base plastered with clay. Around this there was a terracotta channel to drain away the excess metal and melted wax (the 'lost wax' technique was a complex casting process in which wax was melted, hence 'lost'). Some believe that Phidias made the celebrated huge statue of Athena Promachos which was set up on the Acropolis in the Chalkourgeion here.

The Odeion of Herodes Atticus

The most impressive monument on the south slope is undoubtedly the Odeion which Herodes Atticus, scion of a wealthy family from Marathon in Attica, gave to the city in memory of his wife Regilla. This Odeion, the third after those of Pericles on the south slope and Agrippa in the ancient Agora (15 BC) was built between AD 160, the year of Regilla's death, and AD 174, the year in which the traveller Pausanias visited Athens and wrote enthusiastically of the Odeion. According to the ancient sources it was exceptionally lavish and had a wonderful cedar-wood roof. Indeed, it appears that internal sup-

The Theatre of Herodes Atticus in the 19th century. After the destruction it suffered from the Herulians in AD 267, the Roman building was incorporated into the city's fortifications, initially into the Late Roman wall whilst later, in the 13th century, the tall wall of the skene was incorporated into the Rizokastro, the wall that surrounds the foot of the rock. In 1826, during the revolution, the French Philellene Charles Fabvier and his soldiers invaded the Acropolis from the Theatre of Herodes Atticus, to supply its besieged defenders with food and gunpowder.

Aerial photograph of the Theatre of Herodes Atticus, as the theatre built with the funds of Tiberius Claudius Atticus Herodes in the Roman period is known today. Although it has lost some of its former glory, the building, reconstructed in the 1960s, is still a wonderful venue for theatrical, musical and other productions.

ports were not used for the roof over the *cavea* – an exceptional achievement even by today's standards. Also impressive is the *skene*, or stage, the wall of which, preserved to a height of 28 m, was divided into three floors. On the upper floor it had arched openings and on the lower porches and niches in which statues were placed, as was the habit in Roman theatres. Its semi-circular *cavea* was divided into two sections or *diazomata* with 32 rows of marble seats each, for a capacity of 5,000 spectators. The *orchestra* was also semi-circular and dressed with marble slabs. A stairway had been constructed in the east side of the Odeion, linking it to the neighbouring Stoa of Eumenes.

As with the rest of the buildings on the south slope, the Odeion of Herodes Atticus suffered much destruction during the Herulian raid (AD 267). It was restored in 1952-53 and since 1957 the stage-lights have shone once more as the Odeion plays host to many artistic performances.

The sanctuary of the Nymph

A small open-air sanctuary dedicated to the Nymph, patron of marriage and marriage rituals, was discovered to the south of the Odeion of Herodes Atticus during excavations in 1955-1960. Scholars believe that the Nymph was associated with Hera and Aphrodite, patrons of marriage, and it is to this divinity that the famous *loutrophoroi*, the vases used to transport the water for the marital baths of couples about to be married, were dedicated. The sanctuary was founded in the 7th century BC and initially included a precinct and an altar. Archaeologists have discovered hundreds of artefacts here (*loutrophoroi* and various other offerings), demonstrating the important position it had in the life of the city for several centuries. Its few remains are today to be found hidden in amongst the trees, outside the archaeological site of the south slope, right next to the pedestrianised Dionysius Areopagitus Road.

The Acropolis hill from the northwest. In contrast to the south slope, which was the main place of residence and which hosted areas for events, the difficult, inaccessible north side was

*always isolated. Some of the mystery cults of ancient Athens found a home here, on the most
northerly and darkest side of the sacred rock.*

Inscribed plaque found in the sanctuary of Apollo Hypoakraios and dedicated by the secretary Heratonas, with the names of archons within three laurel wreaths. This sanctuary is where, according to one theory, the nine archons of the city were sworn in, although more recent opinion believes this took place on the rock. As the ancient authors inform us it was from this Acropolis sanctuary that the procession of the 'Pythaists', worshippers of Apollo, set off for the sanctuary at Delphi. AD 85/6-94/5. Acropolis Museum, Gallery of the Slopes, NAM 8155.

NORTH AND EAST SLOPES

The route through the north and east slopes is also of particular interest, offering the viewer not only a more complete picture of ancient Athens but also a delightful walk. Here, in addition to the archaic sanctuaries, the springs and the Panathenaic Way, one encounters the remains of more recent eras, such as the city wall of Haseki and the wall of Hypapanti, which was built during the second phase of Ottoman rule and took its name from the homonymous church located in the northwest of the rock.

Klepsydra

The remains of the Klepsydra, the most important well of the Acropolis, survive on the north side of the rock in a cave-like space. The well that was located here, and where the nymph Empedo was worshipped, supplied the Athenians with water from very ancient times. The research findings show that the first Klepsydra well-house dates to the time of Kimon, in 470-460 BC. In the post-Byzantine period this area was converted into a small church which survived into the 19th century and was known as the Agioi Apostoloi sta Marmara (Holy Apostles at the Marbles).

Sacred caves of Pan, Zeus Olympios and Apollo Hypokraios

Near the Klepsydra there are three cave openings that are home to three sanctuaries. The first, the most easterly, was dedicated to Pan, the goat-legged god whom the Athenians believed had helped them during the battle of Marathon (his cult was established in Athens after 490 BC, the year of the battle). In the 5th century AD the east section of the cave was converted into a Christian chapel dedicated to Saint Athanasius. The neighbouring cave, which began to be used in the 5th century BC is associated by some scholars with Zeus. The third and last cave, the most westerly, is the sanctuary of Apollo Hypokraios and may have been in use since as early as the 13th century BC. Tradition holds that it was here that the god Apollo made love with Kreousa, daughter of the mythical king Erechtheus, producing Ion, the dynastic founder of the Athenians.

Mycenaean well

The Mycenaean well is located to the west of the above caves, at a depth of 40 m and within a natural crevice that was created when a large section of the rock became detached. In order to reach it, the Athenians would use a protected stairway hewn into the rock and which was constructed of wood on its upper part and of stone on its lower part so that it would not be eroded by the humidity. Its upper section led to the cave entrance in the north slope. Some scholars believe that the stairway of the Mycenaean well was used by the young Arrhephorai so they could reach the sanctuary of Aphrodite and Eros.

Sanctuary of Aphrodite and Eros

An open-air sanctuary in which Aphrodite and her son Eros were worshipped as gods of reproduction and fertility. The sanctuary was identified through two inscriptions carved into the rock, one referring to the festival of Eros on the fourth day of the month of Mounichion (late spring) and the other referring to Aphrodite. Excavations here have brought to light a variety of finds, such as fragments of marble sculptures and reliefs, vases, statuettes and stone votive phalluses. Some scholars have associated the sanctuary with the festival of the Arrhephoria described by the 2nd-century AD traveller Pausanias.

Sacred cave of Agraulos

The city's largest cave, on the east slope of the Acropolis. In 1980 an inscribed marble stele was discovered here, dating to 247/6 or 246/5 BC and with a decree in honour of Timokriti the priestess of Agraulos (today housed in the Acropolis Museum). The cave was thus identified with the sanctuary of Agraulos, which research had until then associated with a cave on the north slope. According to the myth, Agraulos, a daughter of king Kekrops, willingly sacrificed herself after a prophecy, throwing herself from the walls of the Acropolis in order to save Athens from a siege that had lasted many years. As tradition tells us, Athenian youths would gather at the sanctuary of the brave girl as soon as they had completed their 18th year in order to swear that they would be willing to defend their homeland till death. According to the ancient historian Herodotus, it is from the cave of Agraulos that the Persians invaded the Acropolis in 480 BC.

Votive relief dating to the early 5th century BC and known as the 'relief of the Graces' as, according to one hypothesis, it represents Hermes playing a double flute and the three graceful daughters of Zeus, the Charites or Graces, dancing. Another interpretation holds that Hermes leads and is followed by the daughters of Kekrops: Pandrosos, Herse and Aglaurus. In this interpretation, Aglaurus holds the hand of a young Erichthonius, mythical king of Athens. Athens, Acropolis Museum, Level I, Archaic Gallery, Acr. 702.

Part of the archaeological site of the South Slope with the Theatre of Dionysus, and further behind the Acropolis Museum, integrated within the urban fabric of the city.

There is no architecture without a concept, an overriding idea that gives coherence and identity to a building. The idea, the concept is what distinguishes architecture from simple construction and not the form.

B. Tschumi, 2004

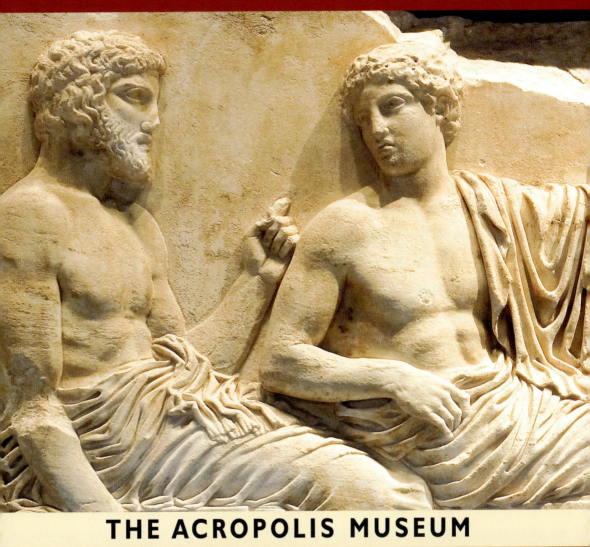

THE ACROPOLIS MUSEUM

The building

In the shadow of the Acropolis, in the historic neighbourhood of Makri-yianni there rises an imposing building that was designed with a double purpose: to display the masterpieces of antiquity and the dialectical relationship with the Parthenon, one of the major monuments of the global cultural heritage.

 The new Acropolis Museum is a building that has been long await-ed, having been opened decades after the need for a new museum

The old next to the new: the new Acropolis Museum and, in front of it, the historical Weiler building. The coexistence continues inside the Museum, where the combination of modern materials and design interacts creatively with the classical beauty of the works of ancient art.

dedicated to the sacred rock was realised. The first architectural competition for the construction of the new Acropolis Museum was held in 1976 and the second in 1979; neither competition was successful. The third competition, announced in 1989, was won by Nicoletti and Passarelli, but the project never progressed due to the discovery of a densely-built section of the ancient city with successive building phases in that part of Makriyianni that had been selected for the museum. The Organisation for the Construction of the New Acropolis Museum was subsequently established and, in 1994, the matter reached its final stages. The fourth international architectural competition was won by the Swiss architect Bernard Tschumi in collaboration with the Greek architect Michel Photiadis, and the new museum was finally built.

The specifications which the competing architecture firms had to fulfil were very particular: the new museum had to incorporate the excavation of the ancient quarter so as to make it visible to visitors; natural light had to be used so as to give the sense of open space; there was to be a balanced relationship between the Museum's architecture and the ancient monuments on the Acropolis rock; and the building had to be satisfactorily integrated with the immediate and broader urban environment and enable the visitor to see both the architectural sculptures of the Parthenon and the Parthenon itself on the Acropolis at the same time. The building that was constructed responds inventively to all the above requirements. The core of its conception was three successive yet independent levels (base, middle and top), a composition of almost mathematical precisions. Supported on 43 free-standing columns, the Museum is essentially suspended above the excavation, offering the visitor an impressive view of the ancient remains, while the widespread use of glass allows communication with the external environment and the use of the natural light in order to showcase the exhibits. Drenched in the Attic light, the superb sculptures of gods, maidens, youths and horsemen in the double-height Archaic Gallery, are freely arranged and compose a vibrant whole, a modern 'Agora', where people and sculptures mingle and the appearance of which changes according to the time of day. Light plays an equally important role in the area created to house the sculptural decorations of the Parthenon. This Gallery, built almost completely of glass, is located on the upper level of the Museum, and its axis has been rotated so as to make it parallel with the ancient temple. The exhibits have been installed in such a way as to resemble the Parthenon, and the sculptures thus have the same orientation and arrangement as they had when on the temple, bathed in light at the same corner.

The materials used in the Acropolis Museum are simple and modern: concrete, steel and, as mentioned above, plenty of glass, which was also used in the flooring to create a visual continuity between the Parthenon Gallery and the excavation at the foot of the Museum. Marble was selected for the floors: black marble of Macedonia for the general and circulation areas and beige from Mt Helicon for the exhibition areas, to match with the patina of the sculptures.

Harmonious too is the coexistence of the new museum with the preserved building of the Centre for Acropolis Studies, known as the Weiler building after the German engineer Wilhelm von Weiler who

built it. Constructed in 1836, it was originally used as a military hospital.

The new Acropolis Museum was opened with much fanfare in June 2009, and contains 14,000 square metres of exhibition areas, as well as a virtual reality theatre, an auditorium and areas for temporary exhibitions. It also has a restaurant, gift shops, workshops, a garage, storerooms and other auxiliary areas, covering a total area of approximately 23,000 square metres. Its great size as well as its excellent design strengthen Greece's voice in the call for the repatriation of the 'Elgin marbles', the antiquities that Lord Elgin had removed from the Acropolis in the early 19th century and which are today found in the British Museum.

View of the Acropolis Museum. The main feature of the building, which dominates the surrounding area, is the widespread use of glass so as to make the best use of the brilliant Attica light.

The archaeological excavation

Openings outside and glass floors inside and outside secure visual contact with the excavation over which the Acropolis Museum was built. In the photograph, one of the characteristic images of this excavation: the round hall-tower of a Byzantine building dating to the 7th century AD.

As you walk down the large stairway that leads to the building, you will get a first, impressive glimpse of all that was hidden and remains hidden within the earth, beneath the feet of today's Athenians. The excavation at the foot of the Museum has revealed an entire neighbourhood of ancient Athens, with its houses, roads, baths and workshops. This neighbourhood developed to the south of the Acropolis from the late Neolithic period until around the 12th century AD. Most of the archaeological remains that you see today, however, date to the period of late antiquity and the early Byzantine period. Some of the most ancient remains can be seen peeking out amongst them.

Visitors will soon have the opportunity to walk through this ancient Athenian neighbourhood, and it is anticipated that a separate museum dedicated to it will be opened. Until then, however, this charming picture of the past is visible only from high above, through the openings and the glass floor in the ground level of the Museum. From the large opening in the covered entrance one can see a large Byzantine church of the 7th century AD, with several rooms, wells, cisterns, private baths and a characteristic circular tower room. This same building can be seen along the length of the north side of the Museum, as well as beneath the glass floor of the foyer, whilst the glass floor of the interior lobby covers a much older building, a residence of the 5th century BC. Here it is worth observing the room with the mosaic floor, which according to the specialists was the *andron*, the symposium room where the head of the house would welcome his male friends and acquaintances for a meal, to philosophise, play games and entertain themselves.

At the entrance*

The visitor is greeted at the Museum's impressive facade by a sizeable marble owl (*Acr. 1347*, early 5th century BC), set upon a tall pedestal between the entrance and the exit. The owl, the sacred bird of the goddess Athena, is considered even today to be a symbol of wisdom.

The Gallery of the Slopes of the Acropolis

The first Gallery in the Museum houses finds from the slopes of the Acropolis, and the floor of the Gallery is thus built on a slope, in a symbolic representation. The first exhibit, which can be seen lit up in a case set in the floor, after the ticket turnstiles, is of symbolic significance. This is an *engainion*, found beneath the floor of a house excavated at the base of the Museum and which dates to the early 3rd century BC. *Engainia* were the remains of sacrificial ritual pyres lit during the laying of foundations or the renovation of a residence. In order to placate the deities that protected the house, the ancient Greeks would burn animal flesh and poultry in a small pit and dedicate small vessels with offerings, a practice which brings to mind the widespread modern Greek custom of sacrificing an animal, usually a rooster, when building foundations are laid. During the Museum's opening ceremony in June 2009 the final item was placed in this case, a small black-glaze *kantharos* (a wine cup covered with a glossy black slip).

* Note: The exhibit number (on the exhibits in the cases) or Museum catalogue number is given in italics.

Settlement and cemetery on the Acropolis

A tour of this Gallery may start from the large glass cases on the right-hand side, where a variety of objects of daily use are displayed, mementoes of the people who in very ancient times lived on the rock and at the foot of the Acropolis. The majority of exhibits in this display are vases of various types, the most common of which are *amphoras* (large vases with two vertical handles, used to transport and store primarily liquids), *hydriai* (vases with three handles, used mainly to transport and serve water – the name *hydria* comes from the word *hydor*, meaning water in ancient Greek), *kraters* (large vases, used to mix water and wine), *pinakia* (plates), *kylixes*, *skyphoi* and *kanthars* (cups), and *pyxides* (round vessels, used to store cosmetics and jewellery).

First case

The first display contains several undecorated vessels from the initial, Neolithic settlement phase of the Acropolis, and more elaborate ones from the Mycenaean period (1600-1100 BC). Of the latter, the highlights are the *flat alabastron* (vessel for transporting and storing perfumes, *11*, 1500-1400 BC), the *false-mouthed amphora* (stirrup jar, typical Mycenaean vase with a false, closed mouth, *12*, 1500-1460 BC) and the *hydria* (*30*, 1400-1300 BC) on the uppermost shelf. The next section of the case is impressive, including wonderful vases of the Geometric period, an era during which a large section of this area was used as a cemetery. The excavations brought to light graves, burials (children's graves with votives) and urns in which the ashes of the dead who had been cremated were stored. As was the custom in antiquity the dead were accompanied by vases and many other objects, the archaeological term for which is grave goods. Our attention here is drawn to two almost identical, 'twin' one might say, *kraters* (*49-50*), the *cup* (*44*) and the terracotta *beads* (*47*), all from a cremation of 900-850 BC. Above is an *oenochoe* with schematised birds (vase for collecting and serving wine, *58*, from a burial of 750 BC), various types of *pyxides* and the *spinning top* (*65*) from a cremation of the early 8th century BC, the large burial *amphora* with the horses (*73*, jar burial, 720-700 BC), as well as another grave *amphora* this time decorated with birds (*82*, jar burial, 740-735 BC).

Second case

The next case begins with artefacts associated with the commercial and economic life of the inhabitants of the Acropolis. The *half-sculp-*

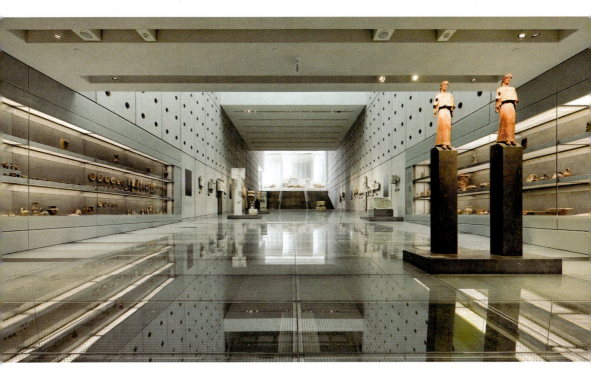

tures (*statuette of the god Pan, head of the god Dionysus, etc.*) and the *moulds* of statuettes and a relief lion show that there had been terra-cotta workshops as well as marble workshops in this area. Of interest are the two *amphora handles* with seals indicating their origins, as well as two *weights*, of *marble* (*10,* 1st-3rd c. AD) and *lead* (*11,* 3rd-1st c. BC). There follows a series of vases and vessels that people used at the table, some simple and for daily use, others luxury, for official dinners and symposia. Exceptional are the two red-figure *kraters*, one portraying a *religious procession* (*74,* 350-325 AD), and the other featuring a *crotalistria* in front of the gods (*crotala* were a percussion instrument played like today's castanets; *75,* late 5th c. BC). A black-figure *olpe* (jug) stands out in the adjacent section of the case, portraying the god of wine *Dionysus, the goddess Athena and Satyrs* (*65,* late 6th c. BC). The last section of this case is dedicated to the children who lived and grew up on the Acropolis hill, their games and the objects they used. Here one can see, amongst other artefacts, the *head of a girl* (*115,* 2nd-1st c. BC), *plangones* (dolls, *118-120,* 5th c. BC), a *lamp in the form of Telesphorus* (mythical demon, son of the god of medicine Asclepius, associated with recovery from illness, *121,* 3rd c. AD), *figurines* primarily of the 5th century BC, a *game in the form of a donkey* (*126*), *miniature pots* and a *miniature mirror* (*102*), *astragaloi* (the ankle bones of small animals with which children played various games, *97-98*), and finally bone *graphides* (styluses with which children

Two almost identical statues of Nike made of dark red clay and found in 1956 at a spring on the North slope of the Acropolis, near the Theatre of Herodes Atticus, along with other artefacts from the Roman imperial period. Their serious faces are reminiscent of works of the severe style, although they are dated to the Roman period on the basis of the rendering of the body and hair. The lower parts of their arms, which according to experts were inset and raised, are missing. The two Nikes are believed to have been used as acroteria, adorning a building of the era. Gallery of the Slopes, Acr. 6476, 6476a.

would write on wax-covered tablets; one end was sharp so as to imprint the letters and the other flat so as to erase them, *104-107*). The uppermost section of the case hosts antefixes (roof ornaments), dating from the 1st to the 3rd century AD.

At this point, in front of the cases, two wonderful terracotta *Nikes* stand on a tall pediment (*Acr. 6476, 6476a*). They date to the 1st-3rd centuries AD and come from the south slope of the Acropolis. They were perhaps used as *acroteria* (ornamental roof antefixes placed at the eaves of the pediments) on a building.

Third case

The third case introduces us first to the ancient world of women. One of the finest artefacts is the giant lid of a red-figure *lekanis*, portraying *Dionysus* and his female followers the *Maenads* (the *lekanis* was a deep plate with a cover and two horizontal handles, used as a food container, a basin for washing, vessel for sacrifices and more; *1*, 4th c. BC). Other interesting exhibits are the bone *perones* (hair and clothes pins, *2*, 3rd-4th c. AD), the bone *comb* (*3*), bone *utensils* (*spatulas, small spoon, 4-7*, 1st-4th c. AD), *spindles* (for spinning, *15-16*, 600-480 BC), *agnythes* (loom weights, *18-20*, 5th-4th c. BC), *perfume unguentaria* (*22-23*, 3rd c. BC), the terracotta *bust of a woman* (5th c. BC, *25*), and the charming *female figurine heads* (*26-27*, 3rd c. BC). Of the pots and vessels that follow, particular attention should be paid to the *filter jug* (vessel similar to the modern jug, this particular one has a perforated strainer for pouring, *90*, 2nd c. BC), *mortars and pestles*, the first from the 2nd-1st c. BC, the other from the 1st-3rd c. AD (*57-60*), the *amphora* with the satirical inscription (*32*, late 6th c. BC) and the *braziers* (terracotta portable hearths for cooking and heating, *71-72*, mid 2nd-early 1st c. BC). This section of the first gallery ends with artefacts pertaining to religious life, such as the lead *magic wheels* (*153-154*), the small terracotta *altar* (*162*, 150-86 BC), and the impressive *censer lid* (*163*, 150-86 BC). In the lower part of this case there is a series of *skyphoi* and *lamps* that were found in a small pit from the 4th century BC and which scholars associate with the custom of the *engainion*, as well as the *sacrifice of the 'house of Proclus'*, which is reminiscent of rituals with a mystery character. Proclus, a celebrated Neoplatonist philosopher of the 5th century AD was born in Constantinople, and spent the majority of his life in Athens, where he died in AD 485. It is believed that a large building that was excavated on the south side of the Acropolis was his house and school. The three final exhibits of this section were found in this house. These are two *reliefs* and a *funerary sacrificial table* (*mensa*), constructed in the 4th century

BC and reused in the 'house of Proclus' to convert a small space within it into a household sanctuary. The altar is decorated with relief representations, mourning on the right side, farewell at the front, a posthumous meeting of the dead man with philosophers on the left side. This subject was obviously considered by the users of the building as commensurate with the building's function as a philosophical school, and for this reason the altar has been placed with this side as its main facade.

Votives from the Sanctuary of the Nymph

Returning to the start of the Gallery, the visitor can admire another splendid group of exhibits. The large cases on the left animate one of life's most important moments: the wedding. The objects which we can see here were found in the small temple on the south slope which the Athenians had dedicated to the Nymph of marriage and wedding ceremonies. The largest section of the cases is taken up by *loutrophoroi*, vases used to transport water for the marital baths of couples who were about to be wed. They are wonderfully decorated with images relating to the wedding and in a style specific to the era. The earlier ones are black-figure, the figures being painted in black 'colour' on a red background with incised details and two levels of 'colour', white and violet. The later vases are in the red-figure style, a later technique of vase paintings born in the Kerameikos quarter of Athens and which is characterised by red figures on a black background. The earlier black-figure *loutrophoroi* feature representations of wedding processions, animals and fantastic creatures, whilst the themes of the red-figure *loutrophoroi* are enriched with mythological scenes and moments from wedding ceremonies. Some of these intriguing vases were large and exceptionally well-made, most probably the offerings of wealthy Athenians. Others, however, were small and simple, reflecting the limited economic ability of their donators. Those which had two handles (*amphora loutrophoroi*) were used for the bridegroom's bath, whilst those with three handles (*hydria loutrophoroi*) were used for the bride's bath.

The *horos* stone (boundary marker) of the sanctuary of the Nymph, dating to 450-400 BC acts as an introduction to this unit. Thanks to this and inscriptions found on the vases, scholars were able to identify this sanctuary even through there are no written references to it, despite its longevity (7th to at least the 2nd c. BC).

First case

Of the wonderful vases in the first case, we can highlight the one decorated with a procession of women in long costumes holding a branch in their hands, Sirens and birds (4, late 7th c. BC), the one with the bride welcoming a procession of women (11, 575-550 BC), and another showing a wedding procession with a four-horse drawn chariot, with a woman charioteer and Apollo in

Black-figure loutrophoros hydria from the sanctuary of the Nymph. On the neck can be seen a procession of women, with chitons and himations, moving towards the right. The body features the scene of the procession also preparing to move towards the right. A woman, the charioteer, climbs onto a four-horse chariot, next to which is Apollo playing the cithar and with an ivy wreath. Behind the four-horse chariot a woman appears to be greeting the procession whilst at the front another woman runs, turning her head back (only the first woman can be seen). Circa 500 BC. Gallery of the Slopes, Votives from the Sanctuary of the Nymph, case I, exhibit 14.

Detail from the body of the black-figure loutrophoros hydria showing the rider climbing up onto the chariot and the wreathed youth, the god Apollo, playing the cithar.

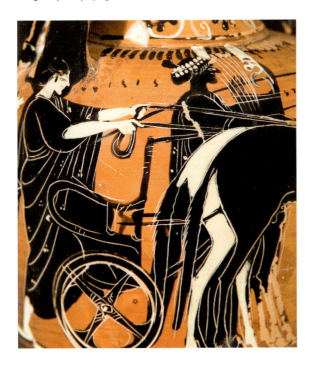

the front holding a *cithar* (*14, ca* 500 BC). It is also worth noticing the *loutrophoroi* with dedicatory inscriptions (*19-22*) in the lower part of the case. These are followed by some other fine *loutrophoroi* and fragments with very interesting representations. On the beautiful exhibit *15* one can see the wedding procession with the participation of the gods Zeus, Hera and Dionysus along with Ariadne, the daughter of the Cretan king Minos (*ca* 550 BC). Vase *9* has a conversation amongst women on its neck (mid-6th c. BC), while *16* features a *loutrophoria* on its neck, and a meeting of men and women on its body (late 6th – early 5th c. BC). The *loutrophoria* was the ritual whereby water was transported to the wedding bath, which took place on the eve of the wedding and the procession of which was led by a young flute-player. Vase *29* (mid-6th c. BC) is adorned with a mythological scene: the Judgement of Paris. The Trojan prince Paris can be seen on the right, with the three goddesses Hera, Athena and Aphrodite to the left, and Hermes in the centre, with his characteristic staff, cap and winged sandals, bringing Zeus's order: Paris should choose the most beautiful of the three goddesses. The next section of this case is dominated by images with a masculine character: a meeting of men and a horseman being led by a youth at *31* (560-550 BC), a procession of men and the Judgement of Paris at *32* (*ca* 550 BC). The neck of *35* (575-550 BC) features a *loutrophoria* while Theseus battles the Minotaur on the body (such scenes appear to have symbolised the virtues of the bridegroom). Exhibit *37* is particularly impressive, featuring a *loutrophoria* with female flute-players and a wedding procession in which the gods Apollo and Hermes participate (*ca* 525 BC).

Second case

In the second case, housing red-figure vases, the presentation of ancient wedding customs continues. The image of a flute-player following a little girl with a *loutrophoros* on her head stands out (*5*, 650-625 BC), as do the representation of a flute-player and a young woman with a *loutrophoros* (*6*, 470-460 BC), the representation of a torch-bearer in a procession (*10*, 470-450 BC) and a series of small fragments, in particular that portraying a female musician preparing her flute (*14*, 425-420 BC). Further along, the visitor will be able to admire scenes from the wedding day itself, when the women dressed the bride and put on her jewellery and her wreath, and the groom would arrive at her house accompanied by his relatives and friends and his *parochos* or *nympheutes*, akin to today's best man. The most beautiful representations here include the moment were the bride is adorned (*16*, 470-450 BC), an adorned bride (*17*, 430-425 BC), and the first time the couple see each other: the bride, wearing a gossamer dress, gazes at the groom, who touches her with his right hand (*28*, 435-420 BC). Other charming scenes are the groom who takes the bride by the hand (*30*, mid-5th c. BC), a beautiful bride with a wreath and veil (*22*, 435-420 BC), a handsome wreathed groom (*20*, 450-440 BC), a groom and a small Eros (*25*, late 5th-early 4th c. BC), the bride and Erotes (*26*, 370-350 BC), and brides completely covered with veils (*31*, mid 5th c. BC; *32*, 470-450 BC). The unveiling: a woman pulls the bride's veil aside in order to reveal her face (*33*, 430-425 BC). A little further along, in the adjoining section of the case, yet another groom takes his wife by the hand (*34*, 445-430 BC). In this section the visitor shall see primarily vases and fragments featuring the wedding procession that accompanied the newlyweds to the groom's house, as well as the *epaulia*, the day following the wedding when the bride received gifts from relatives and friends. These vases included a wonderful representation of a wedding procession with a carriage and the groom holding the reins (*38*, 450-440 BC). Another wonderful representation of a woman has her holding a decorated *loutrophoros* (*43*, ca 430 BC), whilst on another Eros places a wreath on the bride's head, behind whom can be seen another woman holding a casket (*45*, 440-425 BC). Various other exhibits immortalise the wedding gifts: grapes and a fan made of palm leaves (*47*, 425-415 BC); a vase and sash in a woman's hands (*48*, late 5th-early 4th c. BC); elegant chests (*49*, 420-410 BC); a casket and *loutrophoros* upon the head of a woman who holds a small child (*50*, 430-415 BC); and, a basket with wool (*51*, 430-415 BC). Three large, impressive red-figure *loutrophoroi* come next. The first portrays the wedding of Alcestis and Admetus (the mythical Alcestis, model of ideal love, agreed to be sacrificed for her husband; *55*, mid 5th c. BC). The second shows the wedding of the great Pan-Hellenic hero Herakles with Hebe, daughter of Zeus and Hera (*56*, 450-440 BC). The third a groom and bride on a chariot (*57*, 460-450 BC). Next to them it is worth noting the newly-weds gazing into each other's eyes in front of their common home (*60*, 475-450 BC). The luxury *loutrophoroi* of the 4th century BC, decorated with relief figures of the bride, the groom and their entourage provide the epilogue to this case. The elegant heads of the female statuettes and the decoration of these *loutrophoroi* (*70-72*) as well as the wreathed groom wearing a himation with traces of red colouring (*69*) are standouts.

Body of a red-figure loutrophoros with a wedding scene: the groom meets the bride for the first time. The two young people gaze into each other's eyes as he touches her with his right hand. The groom wears a himation as does the bride, although hers is decorated with dots. A piece of material can be seen on the wall between them. Behind them is a woman with torches in her hands and a winged Eros (only the woman behind the bride can be seen). The work dates to 435-420 BC. Gallery of the Slopes, Votives from the Sanctuary of the Nymphs, case 2, exhibit 28.

Third case

The third and final case focuses on the remaining categories of votives from the sanctuary of the Nymphs, including various types of vases, statuettes, busts of women, ritual vessels and miniature imitation vases. Attention is first drawn to the wonderful small *lekythoi*, vases with one handle, a narrow neck and a body that is usually cylindrical. They were primarily used to store aromatic oils for women and athletes but also had other uses, such as grave signs, mainly of women. Their representations feature, amongst other themes, the labours of Herakles (*10-12*, 500-475 BC) and a pottery workshop (*13*, 500-475 BC). Other noteworthy vases here are the alabaster featuring warriors (*31*, 600-575 BC) and the small elegant *aryballoi* – vases for storing aromatic oils for the baths of women and athletes - with representations of warriors (*36-37*, 600-550 BC), and revellers (a group of ridiculous and joyous dancers, *38*, 600-550 BC). Further on, there is a black-figure *loutophoros-hydria* (*2*, 580-575 BC) and some delightful black-figure *skyphoi* (*49-52*, 6th c. BC) with representations of animals and mythical creatures. There are also a *kypellos*, or cup, with a tall foot (*71*, *ca* 600 BC), a wonderful plate with zones of animals and birds (*72*, 6th c. BC), the lid of a *lekanis* with representation of human figures, animals and mythical creatures (*73*, 6th c. BC), the *ritual vessel* with a representation of the daughters of the mythical king Kekrops (*74*, *ca* 540 BC) and a *krater* featuring Amazons (mythical female warriors, *75*, late 5th c. BC). The next section of this case holds some wonderful *plates* of the 6th century BC, including an elaborate one with a representation of Sirens (mythical creatures who were half-woman, half-bird, *78*), one with a lion cleverly positioned on the circular surface (*79*), and one with a rooster and lizard (*80*). Further down one can see *spindle whorls* with painted decoration (*128*, 600-450 BC), *phormiskoi* (terracotta imitation bags for children's games, *132-133*, 570-530 BC), and a *rattle* in the form of a hare (*134*, early 6th c. BC). These are followed by *female heads* and *statuettes* of various periods, as well as a *terracotta ladder*, symbol of Aphrodite Ourania, the patron

Relief votive stele, with a snake wound around it. At the top, standing on a sandal (blaute), is a male figure, perhaps the dedicator, who according to the inscription was called Silon. The sandal has led to the linking of the stele with the 'Hero epi Blaute', who was perhaps worshipped on the southwest slope on the site of the sanctuary of Gaia Kourotrophos and Demeter Chloe (vegetation divinities). Mid-4th century BC. Gallery of the Slopes, NAM 2565.

of marriage (*176*, 6th c. BC). This section ends with a number of excellent terracotta *plaques* of the 6th century BC, such as that with the running deer (*177*), a *kernos* (vessel for ritual offerings, *182*, 700-625 BC), *vases*, including one in the shape of a bull's head (*189*, 560-530 BC) and *statuettes* of animals, birds and a dolphin (550-450 BC).

The Asclepeion, sanctuary of Dionysus and other smaller sanctuaries

The Gallery of the Slopes closes with the two large and other smaller sanctuaries that had been founded on the Acropolis. The area on the left, immediately after the cases containing the finds from the sanctuary of the Nymphs, is dedicated to the sanctuaries of Asclepius, the god of medicine and health, and Dionysus, god of vegetation, intoxication and wine. This very interesting section, which starts with the Asclepeion, opens with the *votive relief inscribed on both sides with the history of the foundation of the sanctuary by the Athenian citizen Telemachus*, 420/419 BC. Next to it we can see the base of a *votive offering* of 320 BC, with a representation of a casket with surgical instruments in relief and two suction cups (*sikyes, NAM 1378*) with, further behind, *relief representations of human body parts*, offerings made by those whom the god had cured. The most intriguing of all these is the *part of a woman's face with inset eyes*, which had been set in the niche of a pillar (*NAM 15244*, second half 4th c. BC). On the wall is a series of very interesting *votive reliefs*, the majority of which are decorated with representations of worshippers approaching Asclepius and his family. The most impressive is that in the form of two unified buildings (*NAM 1377*, mid 4th c. BC). Represented are *Asclepius* and his wife *Epione* along with their daughter *Hygieia*. In front of them are *worshippers leading a sacrificial pig to the altar* (the animal's head can be seen at the bottom, near the legs of the first figure) and transporting a box of gifts. It is also worth talking a closer look at relief *NAM 1341*, from 400 BC, representing a *coachman and wagon approaching Asclepius, Epione and Hygieia*. According to the inscription, it was dedicated by a coachman who had survived an accident in which his wagon, which was transporting stone blocks, was overturned. Of the exhibits from the sanctuary of Dionysus, we can mention the huge *mask* of the god (*Acr. 6461*, 1st c. AD.), the excellent relief *slabs* with ethereal *female dancers* (*NAM 259, 260*, 1st c. BC) and a *statue of Old Silenus* carrying a young Dionysus on his shoulder and a theatrical mask in his hand (*NAM 257*, 2nd c. BC).

Having admired the above items, the visitor can proceed to the

A fascinating exhibit, perhaps dedicated by Praxias, from the sanctuary of Asclepius, god of medicine. This is a section of a marble woman's face with inlaid eyes, which had been inserted into one of the carved niches of a limestone pillar. Second half 4th century BC, Gallery of the Slopes, NAM 15244.

Two plaques with dancers in relief. On one, a young woman turns to the left and lightly raises her rich himation, which flutters imperceptibly, in her hands. The second figure, with a more intense movement, is turned backwards and holds her deep-pleated himation covering her head together in her right hand in front of her neck. It was formerly suggested that they represent two of the three Horai, daughters of Zeus and Themis, personifications of the seasons. These refreshing Ist-century BC creations adorned a monument in the sanctuary of Dionysus. Gallery of the Slopes, NAM 259, 260.

opposite side of the Gallery where finds from various small sanctuaries, founded on plateaus, in caves and on the slopes of the holy rock, are exhibited. The exhibits include *votive reliefs* from the *sanctuary of the Nymphs and Pan* on the south slope: one relief dates to the 2nd century BC (*NAM 1966*) and another to the 5th century BC (*NAM 1329*). Other exhibits include *relief slabs* of the 1st century AD from the *sanctuary of Apollo Hypoakraios* (*NAM 8124, 8123, 8155*) and an unusual *relief stele*, the so-called stele of Silon, named after its dedicator and dating to the mid-4th century BC (*NAM 2565*). The stele fea-

tures a giant relief snake at the top of which the dedicator is represented on a sandal (*blaute*), indicating a connection with the cult of the
'Hero epi Blaute'. In this section of the Gallery, however, the *treasure*
of the sanctuary of Aphrodite Ourania, patron goddess of marriage,
steals the show. On this giant marble 4th-century BC 'money box',
something akin to the money box in Orthodox Christian churches,
newlywed Athenians would deposit a silver drachma coin in the hope
that the goddess would listen to their wishes and grant them a 'life
strewn with flowers'.

Level I: The Archaic Gallery

The imposing stairway at the end of the Gallery of the Slopes, with the giant archaic pediment at its peak, draws the visitor's attention and prepares them for the masterpieces to be encountered on the first floor of the Museum.

The Mycenaean and Geometric Acropolis

A tour of this Gallery starts on the left, with the presentation of the Acropolis in the Mycenaean and Geometric periods. In case 1 you will see typical *Mycenaean vases*, while in case 2, with the *Mycenaean statuettes* and *seals*, the standout exhibits are the *figurine of an ox with rider* (*16*, 1300-1190 BC), an *ox head* (*18*, 1375-1190 BC) and the head of a Sphinx (mythical creature with the head of a woman, body of a lion and wings, *28*, 1300-1190 BC). The third case hosts finds from the Mycenaean fountain, including a *feeder* (dummy, *3*, 1190-1030 BC) and a series of other artefacts (*6-11*, 1375-1190 BC) which have puzzled archaeologists as they cannot conclude whether the Mycenaeans used

them as *buttons, dress weights* or as *loom weights*. Immediately after the visitor will find themselves in front of the so-called the *Coppersmith's Treasure* (in archaeological studies, a 'treasure' is a hoard of valuable objects, such as coins, which their owner hid, often to protect them from an impending catastrophe, and which are discovered again after many centuries). The Coppersmith's Treasure is comprised of a variety of bronze artefacts (ploughshares, daggers, sword, mirror, double-headed axes, etc.) which were found hidden in amongst the stones of a wall and date to 1190-1130 BC. The collection was named the Coppersmith's Treasure as it is believed that it may have belonged to a coppersmith of this particular period. Given the wide use of bronze during the Mycenaean period it is today also described as the Later Bronze Age. In this section of the Museum there is also a model of the Acropolis with the Mycenaean Cyclopean wall, while in a separate case one can see an especially impressive item. This is a bronze disk with *the cut-out figure of a Gorgon*, from the Geometric temple of Athena Polias (the Gorgon was a mythical female monster, with snakes for hair, who would turn anyone who looked her straight in the eye into stone; *NAM 13050*, 7th c. BC).

Reassembled pediment from one of the Parthenon's predecessors, the so-called Hekatompedon. The dynamic group of the two lions, digging their claws into the bull fallen on the ground is framed by Herakles and the Triton, left, and the three-bodied demon, right. These brilliant works were made using Piraeus limestone. The visual effects are emphasised and complemented by incised and relief details, as well as the lively, simple colours. Circa 570 BC. Level I, Archaic Gallery.

The central image of the great pediment attributed to the Hekatompedon. Carefully made, it presents with great realism the dramatic antithesis between the victorious, the lions, who maniacally tear the victim to pieces, and the powerful but defeated bull, which, exhausted, turns its head. A noteworthy detail is the blood running from the bull's wounds. Level I, Archaic Gallery, Acr. 3 +.

The Archaic Acropolis

The visitor now has the opportunity to travel to the distant, noble archaic period of the Acropolis. The exhibits here are divided into two categories: architectural pieces and sculptures, sculptures which decorated buildings as well as the gift offerings made by the faithful to Athena, the so-called votives. During this period the main offerings on the Acropolis were korai, statues of girls with clothes of lively colours, jewellery, ornate hairstyles and the celebrated archaic smile, sometimes otherworldly and enigmatic, other times friendly and jovial, which is encountered on all sculptures of the 6th century BC. The question of what exactly the korai represent remains unanswered. Some were perhaps priestesses or goddesses, others simply young women. Another important type of votive were the *statues of Hippeis* (cavalrymen), which were perhaps dedicated to the divine members of the Hippeis class (the second most wealthy class in Athenian society; they were named thus as they were able to maintain war horses), associated with the cult of Athena Hippias. Smaller groups of votives are comprised of the *grapheis*, perhaps representing officials (treasurers or scribes), *mythological figures*, the *Nikes* and the *reliefs*. Scattered in amongst them are several votive bases, valuable for their inscriptions which afford us numerous details, such as the name of the dedicator, his profession, and the name of the artist who made the offering. Finally, at the back of this section of the Gallery the visitor can admire some later works, examples of the *severe style*, the stage in between archaic and classical art. The severe style in the history of art begins at the close of the Persian Wars (480/479 BC) and ends with the golden age of the maturation of classical art. In this period sculptures were no longer monolithic and stiff, as archaic works were, but they had movement and a more natural pose, shifting the weight of their bodies to one foot, usually the left. At the same time, with their simpler costumes and the replacement of the archaic smile with an expression of introspection and contemplation, they reflect a new attitude towards life, as this was shaped after terrible experience of the Persian Wars.

The architectural sculpture

The first exhibit the visitor can admire is the reassembled grand poros (limestone) pediment that can be seen from the Gallery of the Slopes, representing *two lions tearing a bull to pieces* in the centre *(Acr. 3+)*. Another impressive group has been located to the left, featuring *Herakles* fighting the *sea monster Triton (Acr. 36+)*, while to the right is the *three-bodied demon (Acr. 35+)*: three bearded men conjoined at the waist in the form of a snake. Scholars believe that all three groups,

The right side of the Hekatompedon: group of three bearded male figures with a common body comprised of snake tails, known as the 'three-bodied demon'. The three figures, two of which are turned to the centre and the third towards the viewer, hold items symbolic of nature (bird = wind, water, fire). As for the identity of this enigmatic creature, some argue that it is Nereus, the sea demon who had the ability to change his shape, whilst others believe that it is Typhon, one of Zeus's most dangerous rivals. Level I, Archaic Gallery, Acr. 35+

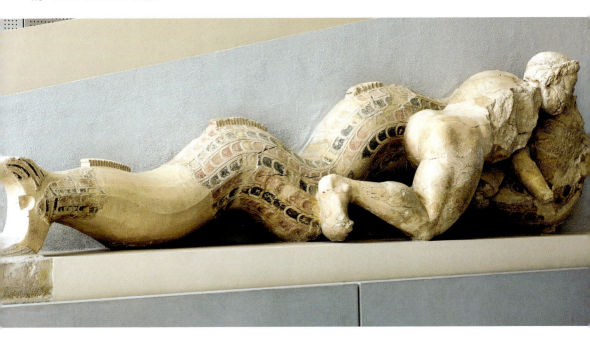

The group that adorned the left edge of the grand Hekatompedon pediment: the great hero Herakles fights with Triton, a mythical sea creature with the upper body of a man and the tail of a fish. Level I, Archaic Gallery, Acr. 36+

along with sections from the *top sima* (gutter), the *raking sima* and the *raking geison* (gutter and geison above the pediment) which flank them (Acr. 4572+), come from the so-called Hekatompedon, one of the forerunners of the Parthenon, dating to approximately 570 BC. The other pediment from the same temple features the stunning scene of a *lioness tearing a small bull to pieces* (Acr. 4+), as well as two imposing *snakes* (Acr. 37+, 40+). A splendid piece is exhibited next to the lioness, also attributed to the Hekatompedon, although not from its pediments but its metopes. This was the *four-horse carriage* (Acr. 575+), which would have been represented along with its rider, in relief or painted on the background of the metope that is today lost. Sections of two *relief panthers* (Acr. 552+) have also been ascribed to the metopes of the Hekatompedon. A detailed plaster model of the Acropolis as it would have been in the pre-classical period can be seen nearby.

Opposite, on the left side of the Gallery, are architectural pieces and pediments from the smaller buildings on the Acropolis, which may have stored votive dedications to the sanctuary. Two of the most significant are inspired by the life and labours of Herakles. The first is of the *pediment* of the *Apotheosis* (Acr. 9, 55), i.e. the reception of the hero to Mt Olympus after his death (another possibility is that this group adorned one of the pediments of the Hekatompedon). Seated on an ornate throne with his wife Hera at his side, Zeus welcomes his beloved son to the divine mountain. The hero, dressed in a short chiton and characteristic lion skin, is followed by Iris, the messenger to the gods, while the now ruined figure in front of him was perhaps his patron Athena. The second pediment (*Acr. 1*), behind the first one, shows *Herakles* battling with the *Lernaian Hydra*, a many-headed monster, and is dated, as is the other pediment, to *ca 570 BC*. The hero's nephew, Iolaos, can be seen on the left side, while the composition also features a large sea crab, an ally of the Hydra. Of particular interest is the *pediment of the Olive Tree or of Troilos (Acr. 52)*, which one can see further in front on the same left-hand side of the Gallery. The mysterious scene, with the building, the figure with the impressive red garment and the carved tree branches on the left is interpreted as either the murder of Troilos, son of the Trojan king Priam, by Achilles, or as a ritual procession to the sanctuary of the goddess Athena (560-550 BC).

The next stop is the grandiose sculptures of the *Gigantomachy pediment* from the 'old temple' of Athena Polias (525-500 BC), taking up almost the centre of the right side of the Gallery, near the wall. A huge Athena in the centre crushes her enemy, the giant Enceladus, a mythical figure associated with volcanic eruptions and earthquakes. Another Giant on the right struggles to get up, supporting himself on his shield which is now lost, while a further two Giants, kneeling on one leg, adorn the corners. This composition is important for the development of architectural sculpture, as the figures are now in the round and not simply in relief as before. Especially impressive is the *lion's head sima*, also from the 'old temple', to the left of the pediment, near the information board (*Acr. 69*). To the right of the pediment one can see two relief slabs from 525-500 BC, one with a representation of Hermes (*Acr. 1343*) and the second with a divine charioteer (*Acr. 1342*). As the information label tells us, sections of relief frieze slabs with divine figures at an Agora (conference) of the gods have been identified as decoration from the old temple.

Small head of a kore, the masterpiece known as the Polos Kore (the polos was a tall crown). This figure, with its oval face, finely delineated lips and dreamy gaze, was produced in circa 500 BC, an era of inner exploration of the Attic spirit and a degree of doubt as to man's abilities. Level 1, Archaic Gallery, case 10, Acr. 696.

Cases

After this and before turning to the ancient votives the visitor may admire the exhibits in the cases on the wall. Case 5 hosts *terracotta roofs*, while the next case contains *pieces from the decoration of the Hekatompedon*: sections of the poros *pedimental cornice*, painted with waterfowl, as well as an impressive poros *owl* and a *snake*, both symbols of Athena. In case 7, with the *terracotta sculptures*, attention is drawn primarily to the statuette of Herakles (*3, ca 500 BC*) and the *antefixes* with the fearsome figure of a *Gorgon (5-6, 510-500 BC)*.

Panoramic view of the Archaic Gallery.

'Smiles and curves, alive inside you, beneath the fearsome gods and the monsters of the old pediments... Pieces of bodies which still breath, show all that was done better and later and always, I presume in Greece.'

George Seferis, *Days III*, Athens: Ikaros, 1977

There follows a case with excellent terracotta pieces, such as the fragments of a *lebetas* (a vessel used to mix wine and water), decorated with, amongst other themes, a Gigantomachy (battle of gods and giants) and the signature of Lydos as vase painter and potter; the visitor can see his name on the large fragment with the monstrous head of a Giant (555-540 BC). Also, the fragments of a *dinos* (wine vessel) signed by the vase painter Sophilos, featuring the wedding of the mortal king Peleas with the immortal Nereid Thetis, the parents of Achilles (*ca* 580 BC) and a *plate* again by the vase painter Lydos, representing the battle between the great Athenian hero Theseus and the man-eating Minotaur (550-540 BC). In case 9 one can see some lovely *archaic marble sculptures*, in 10 and 11 some wonderful korai heads and in case 12 parts of *archaic sculptures*, such as the impressive hand of a sculpture with a shield decorated with the head of a Gorgon (*4, ca* 500 BC). Cases 13 and 14 are dedicated to the *bronze tripod lebetes*, a votive offering usually made at the great Pan-Hellenic sanctuaries from the Geometric to the classical periods. Case 15 is dedicated to *weapons*, including some *sauroters* (the metal spike at the butt-end of a spear, also used as a sharp point when the spear broke, *1-3*, 5th c. BC). Case 16 hosts *bronze male statuettes* and case 17 *bronze offerings to Athena*, as well as an interesting *inscription dedicating vases* from the sanctuary treasurers (*13, ca* 550 BC). The following case contains sections of bronze vases, wonderful artworks, such as the *decoration of a handle with lions tearing a small animal to pieces* (*7*, ca 540 BC) and the *handle of a strainer in the shape of a duck* (*13*, 460-450 BC). Also of interest is case 19, on the subject of *mythological creatures and other votives*. Standouts here are the *stool* (*1, ca* 480 BC), the larger-than-life *eyelid* (*9*, late 6th-early 5th c. BC) and a fine *Pegasus-handle decoration* (Pegasus was the winged horse of the hero Perseus, who beheaded the deadly Medusa, or Gorgon, *11*, 550-450 BC). Exhibited in case 20 following are *animals* and *miniature vases*, in case 21 *terracotta statuettes* as well as a small *doll with moving parts* (*33*, mid 6th c. BC), in case 22 *terracotta heads of women*, in case 23 a few impressive *terracotta statuettes of Athena* and *seated goddesses*, and in case 24 *terracotta statuettes of women*. Finally, case 25 offers the visitor the opportunity to admire one of the finest archaic pieces from the Acropolis: a *terracotta plaque*, perhaps a votive or a section of architectural decoration, featuring a *hoplitodromos* (athlete who took part in foot races wearing his armour). The inscription on the upper part originally read 'Megakles kalos', i.e. Megakles is handsome, although this name was later changed to Glaucytes (*Acr. 67*, 510-500 BC). The two final cases feature *votive plaques with Athena* and *votives with Athena and other divinities*. Standouts in case 26 include a beautiful representation of

Athena in a chariot with Hermes by her side (*11*, late 6th c. BC), an *Athena Promachos* (*13*, ca 500 BC) and *Athena in a temple* (*15*, late 6th c. BC) and in case 27 two relief plaques with a *woman spinning* (*1-2*, 490-480 BC), a painted plaque with a *woman weaving* and a girl seated behind her (*3*, ca 570 BC), and a small *loom weight with the image of an owl* (*5*, 5th c. BC), as well as a further two painted plates, one with *Herakles, Athena* and Herakles' nephew *Iolaos on a chariot* (*6*, early 5th c. BC), and the other with *Herakles, Hermes,* and the *chariot of Athena* (*7*, ca 510 BC).

A little further ahead, in a separate case, stands a giant *black-figure dinos* (vessel used to mix wine with water, *NAM 15116*). This is a work by the artist known as the Painter of Acropolis 606, and dates to 570-560 BC. On its surface are painted, at the bottom, animals and mythical creatures and, further up, military scenes with chariots and horsemen, some armed with spears and others with bows.

The votives

To the right of the pediments of the Apotheosis and the Hydra, the visitor will encounter one of the most famous archaic votives on the Acropolis, the famous *Moschophoros* (*Acr. 624*, 570 BC).

Marble votive Sphinx, a mythical creature with the head of a woman, the body of a lion and wings. This wonderful figure, with its characteristic archaic smile, is dated to 560-550 BC. Level I, Archaic Gallery, Acr. 630.

According to an inscription on its base, this vibrant, smiling statue of a bearded man with a small calf over his shoulders was dedicated to the goddess by '[R]ombos, son of Palos'. A little further to the right two wonderful *Sphinxes* have been set up opposite each other, one dating to 540-530 BC (*Acr. 632*) and the other to 560-550 BC (*Acr. 630*), and further in front a series of beautiful korai. These include the *Lyons Kore*, with the dove in her right hand and which ushered in the fashion for Ionian costume (chiton and diagonal himation) to Athens (*Acr. 269*, ca 540 BC) and the *Peplophoros Kore*, named thus for the simple Doric *peplos* she wears (*Acr. 679*, 530 BC). A wonderful statue of a *hunting dog* has been set up near the Peplophoros (*Acr. 143*, ca 520 BC). A little further down, next to the column of the Gallery, discreetly stands the small-built, joyful *Girl from Chios* (*Acr. 675*, 510 BC). To her right the largest and most famous of the archaic horsemen, the *Rampin horseman* (*Acr. 590*, 550 BC) stands tall. Georges Rampin was the name of the collector who purchased the horseman's head and in 1896 donated it to the Louvre, where it remains until today, whilst the important yet unknown creator of this group is conventionally named the Rampin Master. The wreath of oak or wild celery leaves from the youth's well-made head indicates he was the victor of an athletic contest. Another exceptionally important horseman is located further to the left. Of this one, only the lower part of his body and legs survive, enough to suggest his eastern dress, of a short chiton with painted palmettes and trousers with rhombuses, giving him his name: the

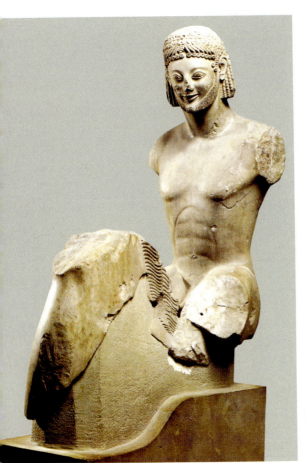

One of the most important Attic works of the mid-6th century BC. The naked young horseman, with a calm and joyful face, in one hand holds tightly onto the now lost reins of his horse and smiles benevolently. His head is a plaster cast. The original, which is housed in the Paris Louvre, is part of the Rampin collection and this outstanding archaic statue thus took the name the Rampin Horseman. Other works from the Acropolis are also attributed to the leading sculptor who created it, such as the famous Peplophoros Kore (Acr. 679) and the lion's head gutter from the 'old temple' (Acr. 69). Level I, Archaic Gallery, Acr. 590.

The Moschophoros is an exceptional Attic creation from the archaic period, carved in grey Hymettus marble. It represents a bearded man carrying a calf over his shoulders as an offering to the goddess Athena, fulfilling in this way one of his vows. This is not a colossal statue, as the earlier archaic statues were, whilst the face of the dedicator, with its lively, expressive gaze and friendly smile, radiates joy. 570 BC. Level I, Archaic Gallery, Acr. 624.

The Peplophoros Kore, a masterpiece with a cheerful mood and vibrantly painted penetrating eyes. She wears a long chiton with delicate pleats below and, above, a peplos formerly attached to the shoulders with metal clasps. Her ears were adorned with earrings (the openings can be seen). Studies have shown that the lower part of the Peplophoros's costume, which was decorated with vertical rows of animals, portrayed Artemis (goddess of hunting), with an arrow in her right hand and a bow in her left. The Peplophoros is believed to be the work of a fine Athenian artist, perhaps the same individual responsible for the Rampin Horseman and other archaic sculptures on the Acropolis. 530 BC. Level I, Archaic Gallery, Acr. 679

This kore strongly reflects the Ionian character and Ionian grace and joie de vivre, which in that period had captivated Athens. She wears an Ionic chiton and a slanting himation fixed to her shoulder, with a crown in her hair that was once adorned with inset metallic jewels and disk-shaped earrings in her ears. This is a particularly fine creation of the late 6th century BC. In the past this kore had been linked to an inscribed column signed by an artist from Chios, and was thus named the 'Girl from Chios'. 510 BC. Level I, Archaic Gallery, Acr. 675.

Tall and proud, with a bright smile this strange kore from the Acropolis exudes self-confidence and nobility. The flirtatious figure with the ornate hairdo, rich costume with a great variety of pleats, characteristic eyes inset with a material that is now lost, long, sharp nose and dimpled cheeks are strongly reminiscent of Ionian works.
She is a genuine representative of the laughing, carefree generation who enjoyed the prosperity of Peisistratid rule before Kleisthenes' takeover. 520 BC. Level I, Archaic Gallery, Acr. 682.

This smiling kore cheerfully raises her dress with her left hand. She wears only a chiton and is an interesting variation on the statues of this series, all the others of which wore a chiton and a himation. Her tender, almost childish face is framed with ringlets, whilst her head is adorned with an ornate crown. Traces of painted decoration can be distinguished on her clothes. 520-510 BC. Level I, Archaic Gallery, Acr. 670.

Euthydikos, the son of Thaliarchos, dedicated this kore to Athena, as an inscription surviving at the base of the statue informs us. The serious, almost melancholy Euthydikos Kore is dressed in an Ionic chiton and slanting himation, although without rich pleats. Also in contrast to the other korai she wears no jewellery, just a ribbon around her long hair. This simple and unadorned figure leaves archaic tradition behind, standing on the threshold of a new era in art and in every aspect of life. After 480 BC. Level I, Archaic Gallery, Acr. 686, 609.

Slender kore with an indiscernible smile and thoughtful look. Both arms were bent at the elbows and stretched out in front, in contrast with most of her sisters, who kept one arm by the side of their garments. In her left hand she held a bird, most of which has been lost along with the lower part of her arm. She wears a chiton, himation and crown on her vibrant red hair. 500-490 BC. Level I, Archaic Gallery, Acr. 685.

Kore dated to circa 500 BC, the work of an important artist of the late archaic period. She too wears a chiton, himation and crown in her hair, decorated with a type of meander, a motif that is repeated along the edge of her himation and the fringe of her chiton. Her smile has almost been wiped from her lips and her slitted, thoughtful eyes, intimations of the 'severe style', distinguish her from her joyful sisters. Experts have named her the 'kore with almond eyes', the 'melancholy kore' and the 'kore with the eyes of a Sphinx'. Level I, Archaic Gallery, Acr. 674.

Persian or *Scythian* (*Acr. 606*, 520-510 BC). The surrounding space is taken up by other *horsemen, votive bases*, including, in the corner, a *workshop scene* (*Acr. 3705*, 550-525 BC), and *korai*, one of which draws our attention, a little one with a dove in her hand and *pointed red shoes* (*Acr. 683*, 510 BC).

Further down, at a central point exactly opposite the Athena of the Gigantomachy, another Athena stands. This is the *Endoios Athena*, a particularly eroded seated statue which has been identified as the famous piece by Endoios, one of the greatest sculptors of the late 6th century BC, well known from the literary sources (*Acr. 625*, 525 BC). Proceeding now towards the left side of the Gallery the visitor will encounter the monumental *Antenor Kore* (*Acr. 681*, 525-510 BC), as well as the *Potter relief*, a relief stele adorned with a seated male fig-ure holding *kylixes*, a piece that has been associated with the potter Pamphaios (*Acr. 1332*, 520-510 BC). Also here are the *scribes*, hunched over their work for centuries (*Acr. 629, 144, 146*, 510-500 BC). A lit-tle further in front one can see a very tall *inscribed column with a stat-ue of Athena* (*Acr. 136+, 6506*, 510 BC), a *kore with the eyes of a Sphinx* (*Acr. 674*, 500 BC), and a beautiful *horse* without a rider (*Acr. 697*, 490 BC). The *Nike of Callimachus*, directly opposite the *lion's head sima* from the 'old temple', dominates as it stands upon the tall, fragmen-tary surviving column. This was a votive dedicated by the family of the Athenian warrior who lost his life at the battle of Marathon (*Acr. 690*, 490-480 BC).

Proceeding, it is worth staying a little at the large case near the statues of the Gigantomachy, with items upon which the traces of the destruction wrought on the Acropolis by the Persians can clearly be seen, as well as a *treasure* comprised of *63 silver tetradrachms* from 483-480 BC. This was a time during which it had been decided, fol-lowing a proposal from the Athenian general Themistocles, that Athens would use the new silver deposits that had been found at mines in Lavrion in order to build a strong fleet, able to take on aspir-ing conquerors. Next to it is the famous *relief of the Charites* (*Acr. 702*, early 5th c. BC), while opposite it are displayed some of the finest works of the severe style, the early period of classical art: the *Kritios Boy* (*Acr. 698*), the *Blond Boy* (*Acr. 689*) and the *Euthydikos Kore* (*Acr.*

Front section of a horse, without a rider, wonderfully preserved. This animal, so beloved by the ancient Greeks, is represented here all movement and vibrancy. It may, experts believe, have belonged to a sculptural group of horses. Circa 490 BC. Level I, Archaic Gallery, Acr. 697.

This 'Persian' or 'Scythian' horseman is one of the most important statues of a horseman from the archaic Acropolis. Numerous fragments were rejoined and filled in with plaster in order to bring the statue to its present form, which is more complete than in the past. The horseman, seated on his horse with its erect mane and straight neck, wears a belted short chiton and trousers in garish colours and designs. The bronze nails at his feet held sandals, which are now lost. In the past, because of the similarity between the horseman and a painting in Oxford bearing the inscription 'Miltiades kalos', it was claimed that the statue represented the famous Athenian general Miltiades, who lived in Thrace in the late 6th century BC. 520-510 BC. Level I, Archaic Gallery, Acr. 606.

The Potter relief, obviously the dedication of a potter or vase painter, as can be seen from the two kylixes that he holds in his left hand. The man, seated on a stool, wears a himation that leaves the upper part of his body bare – as befits an artisan, who needs to be able to move freely. On his face, with its pointed beard, straight nose and fleshy lips, an intense, wilful personality can be seen. It is believed that a painted representation must have occupied the empty space on the left. Some experts believe that the relief was a work of the Athenian sculptor Endoios. 520-510 BC. Level I, Archaic Gallery, Acr. 1332.

In the late 6th century BC three scribes seated on stools were dedicated on the Acropolis. In the photograph the largest (Acr. 629) writes with his stylus, which was metal and is now lost, upon a slab which had formerly been attached with joints to his thighs. His face is a copy of the original fragment housed in the Louvre (Fauvel head). Researchers believe that the scribes of the Acropolis represent state officials, perhaps sanctuary treasurers or secretaries of the demos, an office established with the foundation of democracy in Athens. 510-500 BC. Level I, Archaic Gallery.

686, 609), all dating to after 480 BC. In the next case one can see a fine *bronze hoplite head* (NAM 6446, 480-470 BC) and in the opposite case an exceptional *bronze statuette of Athena Promachos* (NAM X6447, 475 BC), dedicated to the goddess by Meleso as a *dekate*, a tenth of an income of hers, as well as a wonderful *double-faced bronze sheet with the figure of Athena* (NAM X6448, 530 BC). Some of the more interesting exhibits in this corner are the *Propylaia Kore* with her red hair (Acr. 688, 480 BC), the *Angelitos Athena* (Acr. 140, 480-470 BC) and the relief of *Mourning Athena* (Acr. 695, 460 BC). At this point, the imaginary historical route followed by the visitor leads to the next level, where the most beautiful work of art and architecture of the high classical period is exhibited: the Parthenon.

Front and side views of an exceptional work of the severe style: the Blond Boy. It is thus named because its hair was discovered to have had a bright gold colour. It is worth observing the hair-style, with the braids that cross at the nape and become lost, a little above the ears and beneath the long ringlets over the forehead. The structure and shape of the head, which are completely different from those of archaic sculptures, indicate a deep spirituality in the youthful, almost melancholy figure. After 480 BC. Level I, Archaic Gallery, Acr. 689.

The Mourning Athena sculptural ▶ relief is one of the masterpieces of the Acropolis Museum. The goddess is depicted on a once blue background wearing an Attic Doric peplos and Corinthian helmet, supporting herself on her spear and bowing her head in thought. Various theories have been proposed for the rectangular stele in front of her, such as that it might be a horos stone (marking the boundary of her sanctuary), a tomb stele or a list of accounts for her sanctuary. Characteristic of the art of this era is the figure's inner world and the artist's attempt to portray emotions. 460 BC. Level I, Archaic Gallery, Acr. 695.

*Statue of a naked youth, which has been linked
to the sculptors Kritios and Nesiotes, and is thus
known as the Kritios Boy (Kritios and Nesiotes
were the creators of the Tyrannicides group of
Harmodius and Aristogeiton, the two Athenians
who killed Hipparchus the son of the tyrant
Peisistratus and which is known from Roman
copies). This is one of the finest examples of the
'severe style'. The stance of the body, with the
straight left leg and relaxed right leg, breaks with
tradition and acts as a prelude to the artistic
achievements of the late classical period.
After 480 BC. Level I, Archaic Gallery, Acr. 698.*

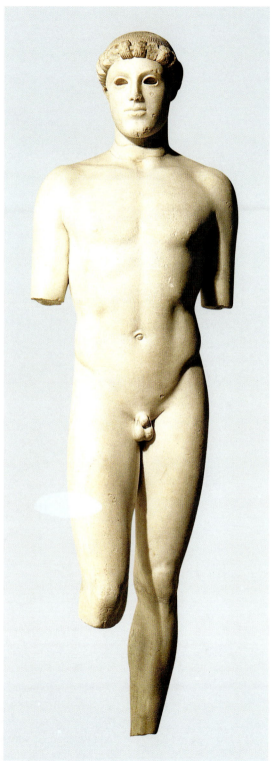

The Parthenon Gallery

In the vestibule one can see the reconstructions, on a miniature scale, of the two pediments of the temple, designed by the Austrian sculptor Karl Schwerzek (1904), a model of the Acropolis during the classical period and several interesting *inscriptions*. Of these, we can indicatively mention the *honorary vote on the Ergastines*, the Athenian girls who for nine months would weave the *peplos* cloak of the statue

The Parthenon Gallery is in direct visual contact, as was the goal, with the sacred rock in the background. It should be noted that the casts of the sculptures that are today in the British Museum were sent to Greece by Great Britain in 1846 after a request from the Greek government. They were initially displayed in the old Acropolis Museum, subsequently displayed in the Centre for Acropolis Studies and, finally, used to complete the image of this masterpiece of antiquity in the new Acropolis Museum.

of Athena (*NAM 7665/6 + NAM 8090, 103/2 BC*), and the *account of the expenses for the production of the chryselephantine statue of Athena by Phidias,* which adorned the cella of the Parthenon (*NAM 6769, 438 BC*). In addition, a documentary on the construction and history of this famous temple can be seen in a special area.

In the central Gallery, which has the same orientation and dimensions as the Parthenon, are exhibited the *pediments* (those figures that have survived), the *metopes* and the *frieze*. These include both original

The southwest corner of the Parthenon Gallery. In this creatively designed gallery the exhibits have been positioned with the same orientation and arrangement as in the ancient temple. The pedimental sculptures are on the first level. Behind and at a higher level are the metopes, and even further behind the metopes and the metal columns, reminiscent of the temple's peristyle colonnade, is the frieze. The blocks of the frieze, originals and copies, have been set relatively low − in contrast with their position on the Parthenon, where they were very were high up − so that visitors can admire them in all their detail and beauty.

pieces and plaster casts, as a large portion of the temple's sculptural decoration was acquired by Lord Elgin and today adorns the British Museum in London. This innovative and brave combination of originals and copies, as well as the cleaning of the works using pioneering technology enable the visitor to better understand this sculptural group and enjoy its beauty.

As the visitor will discover, the greatest damage has been suffered by the *pediments* of the ancient temple. The *metopes* are also particularly damaged, as some of the figures on the west, east and north sides were hacked by the early Christians during the period when the Parthenon was being converted into a Christian church. As if by magic, however, or perhaps because their subjects were given a Christian interpretation, the metopes of the south side were saved, as was the 32nd metope on the northwest corner of the temple. The last one, with two goddesses facing each other, Hera and Hebe, may have been interpreted by the Christians as the Evangelism of the Theotokos (Virgin Mary).

The *frieze*, the masterful representation of the Panathenaic procession, also survives fragmentally. Thankfully, however, modern scholars have the drawings of Jacques Carrey, a member of the retinue of the French ambassador to Constantinople in 1674, available to them. These drawings provide an exact image of the frieze before the great destruction of the Parthenon in 1687. There were only six blocks from the long sides that Carrey did not see: these had been removed to create a window in the Christian church. Some time later, in the mid-18th century, two British architects, James Stuart and Nicholas Revett, produced the first architectural drawings of the temple and of those sculptures which had survived. Destruction struck once more in the early 19th century, when Lord Elgin's people removed the relief surface of numerous blocks using a saw, so as to be able more easily to transport these wonderful images to Great Britain (as only a thin surface remained, these relief representations from the frieze were in the past referred to as 'slabs').

In its position today, in the Museum Gallery bathed in light, the Parthenon frieze is set low, so that the visitor can admire it unobstructed. Its original position, however, was at a height of several metres, in the shadow of the colonnade in the wing, with the result that the blocks could not be seen well. This was counter-balanced with the use of colour, with a bright blue background and the way in which they were carved, making the sculptural surface incline towards the viewer. In response to the question as to whether the frieze was carved before or after it was positioned on the building, most scholars believe it was after for the long sides and before for the west side, where there is an autonomous scene on each block. As for the design, the ancient sculptors brilliantly adapted the size and positions of the 380 human and over 220 animal figures onto this limited space. A characteristic example is the reduced size of the horses, whilst the gods are represented as seated, so that they could be rendered in a large size. Observing the figures now, one can distinguish their common characteristics, such as a relatively broad forehead, long straight nose, fleshy lips, long chin, as well as an expression focused on the procession. Yet, the viewer will also see differences according to age and gender (the older men have beards, the younger men are clean-shaven and usually have short wavy hair; women have their hair tied back). There is also a wide variation in costume and footwear: individual breastplates, chitons, chlamys, himations, sandals with thick soles for women and thin soles for men, boots. Some of the horsemen even wear costumes from other places, Macedonia for example, and Thrace, as well as an *alopekis* (fox-skin cap). The representation of the procession, which starts in the southwest corner of the temple, is divided into two groups going in a different direction – one crosses the south side, the other the west and subsequently the north. Both end on the east side, with the scene of the presentation of the *peplos* cloak, on both sides of which the gods of Olympus are seated, as though welcoming the two sections of the procession.

Section of the west frieze with scenes of preparation and the start of the procession for the Great Panathenaia. The Ionic frieze of the Parthenon has led to endless debate and disagreement amongst scholars, although no one doubts its exceptional composition and flawless execution, perhaps the highest gift of the Athenians to their city's patron goddess, the goddess of wisdom and the arts.

Despite the unity of the subject (Panathenaic procession), the study of the frieze has resulted in many problems of interpretation, as the various scenes are positioned in different places and times. The horsemen on the west side, for example, appear to be at the Dipylon gate, where the procession started, whereas the *skaphephoroi* (youths bearing trays with offerings) had already moved on and presented their offerings. Many questions also remain unanswered as to exactly where the scene with the presentation of the *peplos* took place, and why there is no representation of the Panathenaic ship on the mast of which, as we know from the literary sources, the *peplos* was transported spread out like a sail. Various theories have been proposed. One states that Phidias and his team were carving on the marble an image of the first Panathenaic procession, whilst another identifies the 192 horsemen of the frieze with the 192 heroised fallen at the battle of Marathon. Another view holds that different eras of the Panathenaic procession are being presented (mythical, archaic and classical). Irrespective of the interpretations and questions, however, one fact remains, that the Parthenon frieze, this eternal hymn to the democratic Athens of the 5th century BC, represents a rare moment in the history of art.

The West side

An introduction to the most perfect creations of classical sculpture can start from the west side of the Gallery. The west side was the back side of the temple, but also the first side one saw when entering the Acropolis from the Propylaia.

The pediment

The visitor here will first see the fragments of the *west pediment*, portraying the conflict between Athena and Poseidon, god of the sea, for guardianship over Athens. The contest took place on the rock of the Acropolis, where the gifts of the two gods were preserved until late

antiquity: Athena's olive tree in the Pandroseion, and Poseidon's salty spring in the Erechtheion. The middle of the scene is taken up by the two protagonists, *Poseidon* and *Athena*, flanked by their chariots. The charioteer in Poseidon's chariot was his wife Amphitrite, whilst *Nike* was in Athena's chariot, although she no longer survives. The outer horses on both chariots were supported on two *Tritons*. Here it should be mentioned that the Venetian general Morosini, as though the damage caused by his cannons were not enough, unsuccessfully attempted to remove the horses of Poseidon and Athena, resulting in some of the sculptures falling to the ground and smashing to pieces. Behind the chariots were the two messengers of the gods, *Hermes* on the left and *Iris* on the right (the Laborde head, taken to Venice by Morosini's secretary and now found in the Louvre has been identified as that of Iris), followed by mythical figures of Attica. The group of the seated man and the slender woman embracing him on the left is believed to represent the Athenian king *Kekrops* and his daughter *Pandrosos*, whilst the neighbouring figures are identified as the other *daughters of Kekrops* and his son *Erysichthon*. The snake in between Kekrops and Pandrosos helped to identify Kekrops as the mythical king and he is often represented on vases as half-snake. On the right, behind Iris and Aphrodite, were various figures whom it is believed portrayed *Oreithuia*, daughter of king Erechtheus and wife of Boreas, *Kreousa*, also a daughter of Erechtheus, and her son *Ion*, father of the Ionians. Two almost-reclining figures had been wisely positioned in the corners: on the left a *river god* of Attica, *Ilissus* or *Eridanus*, on the right a personification of the famous Attic spring *Kallirhoe*. The naked kneeling man in front of her must also be a *river god*, perhaps *Ilissus*. The scene was completed by Athena's olive tree, and prevailing opinion believes that it was made of bronze and positioned between the two gods, in the centre of the pediment.

The corner of the Gallery, on the right, is dominated by the colossal *plant acroterion* that crowned the peak of the Parthenon pediment. Its initial height is calculated as 3.90 to 4 metres. The only original part is one of the marble acanthus leaves with the original fragments rendered in colour.

Cast reconstruction of one of the impressive acroteria in the shape of acanthus leaves that adorned the peak of the Parthenon pediment. The following oddity can be observed with the acroteria: around 27 sections of the central plant-shaped acroteria have survived but there is no trace of their bases; with the corner acroteria, however, only their bases have survived, with the result that we cannot be certain of their form. Parthenon Gallery, west side.

The west side of the Parthenon Gallery, with the pediment in the forefront, the metopes further behind and the frieze in the background. Of the pediment statues, the half-reclining river god and the famous group of Kekrops and Poseidon can best be seen. According to the myth, the Athenian king Kekrops was present at the battle between Athena and Poseidon. Pandrosos was the only one of his three daughters who obeyed Athena's order not to open the basket that the goddess had entrusted to them. The other two, Herse and Agraulos (or Aglauros), opened it and, as soon as they saw the serpent-shaped Erichthonius, were driven mad by fear and killed themselves by jumping from the Acropolis rock.

The metopes

The subject of the metopes on the west side, according to most scholars, was the *Amazonomachy*, the mythical battle between the Greeks and the Amazons (Amazons were a mythical martial race of female warriors who lived at the Pontus). It all began when the Athenian king Theseus fell in love with Antiope, queen of the Amazons, and took her with him to Athens. This act brought the fearsome female warriors to the walls of the Acropolis, where they fought bravely, although they were defeated and suffered great losses.

Hacked by the Christians, the west metopes are generally much ruined. The representations on the last two on the southwest and the corner one on the northwest can perhaps be seen a little better. The

View of the west side of the Parthenon Gallery, with the pediment sculptures dominating the photograph. The statues of the two pediments were the largest that had ever been produced in Greece in the classical period and were almost all fully carved in the round, at the back as well. Researchers have estimated, through a study of the ancient sources, that more than one sculpture workshop must have been involved in their creation. In 434/3 BC the sculptors of the pediments received 16,392 drachmas. We do not know if this figure represents their annual salary, but it nonetheless seems astronomical compared to the total cost of 3,010 drachmas per pediment for the admittedly smaller temple of Asclepius at Epidaurus.

last one (*Metope 1*), the only one with just one figure, features a *horse-back Amazon*, with a short chiton and a chlamys flowing behind her as she rushes forward towards the left with her right hand raised, perhaps holding a spear. This figure may have been queen *Antiope*. The remaining metopes show scenes of Greeks and Amazons in pairs, in a variety of positions. As a rule, the Greeks are winning, although in some metopes the female warriors with the legendary skills overpower their enemies.

The frieze

On the west side there is a series of human scenes – someone does up his sandal, someone else fixes his bridle, another strokes his horse

The first metope on the west side of the Parthenon with a galloping Amazon (cast). It is believed that the themes on the temple's metopes (gods against Giants, Greeks against Trojans, Athenians against Amazons, Lapiths against Centaurs) allude to the victories of the Greeks over the Persians, victories which for the 5th-century Greeks represented the defeat of the powers of chaos and hubris and the prevalence of order and harmony.

– portraying with astonishing vibrancy the atmosphere of the preparations for the start of the procession. The procession begins in the southwest corner, at block *W XVI, (30)*, where a marshal prepares to wear his himation. Next to him an assistant attempts to put a bridle over a horse whilst a horseman rests his foot on a rock as he laces up his sandal. A powerful scene follows: a horseman rushes to help his companion, whose horse has bolted and is standing on its hind legs. Further along, on the delightful block *W XII, (22-24)* one can see a herald with his right hand raised – in his left, scholars believe, he held a Hermes staff or trumpet of metal, attached to the drill holes that can be seen on the block – a horseman next to a horse that lowers its head and an assistant with his master's himation thrown over his shoulder. Also impressive is block *W XI, (20-21)*, with a pair of galloping horsemen, one dressed as a hoplite (breastplate and helmet) and the other wearing an *exomida* (a short chiton fastened to one shoulder). A further two horsemen – one strokes his horse – gallop livelily on the next block *W X, (18-19)*, which experts believe may have been a work of Agoracritus. The next block, *W IX, (16-17)*, is particularly noteworthy, in particular the horseman wearing a *petasos* (wide-

Block XII, 22-24 of the west frieze with a herald raising his right hand as a signal that the procession should start, a horseman next to his horse and an attendant with his master's himation over his shoulder. The west frieze, with the exception of blocks I and II which are in the British Museum, remained in its position on the Parthenon until 1993, when it was removed and taken to the Acropolis Museum for protection.

Two horsemen riding on block X, 18-19 of the west frieze, which is believed to have been made by Agoracritus, a famous student of Phidias and one of his collaborators in the creation of the sculptural decoration of the Parthenon. The first horseman wears an anatomical thorax (a cuirass displaying his anatomical details) and the second a chiton and chlamys that flutters behind him.

The image of a horseman wearing a petasos (wide-brimmed hat) on block IX, 16-17 of the west frieze is famous. The man carefully holds onto the reins. In front of him another horseman trots along. The corner of this block, where the hind legs of the horse can be seen, was previously missing. It was then recognised amongst the fragments kept in the storerooms and put back in its place.

The central block of the west frieze (VIII, 15), a masterpiece attributed to Phidias himself. The horseman, who represents either Theseus or one of the two Athenian hipparchs (cavalry commanders), wears an exomida (a short chiton fastened to one shoulder), chlamys and Thracian costume accessories: an alopekis (fox-skin cap) and embades (boots).

Block VI, 11-12 of the west frieze. It represents a youth tying up the sandal on his left foot. Behind him is a horseman with an anatomical thorax, lion-shaped epaulets and a gorgon on his chest. His helmet is decorated with an eagle with a snake in its mouth.

Scene of preparation on block V, 9-10 of the west frieze. One horseman is on his horse, another next to his and holding the reins in one hand and a strigil in his left (a metal implement used by athletes to clean their bodies of the dust, sweat and oil which they rubbed into their skin at the end of training or competitions).

Two further horsemen from block IV, 7-8 of the west frieze. The bearded horseman on this block as well as figure 15 on block VIII are identified by some as the two hipparchs of ancient Athens. Another view holds, on the basis of their Thracian costumes, that they are Thracian allies.

Block III, 4-6 of the west frieze shows a marshal standing in front of a horse and its rider, while further behind an assistant held the reins, which were painted on. A fragment of this block, the assistant's hand, is in Munich.

The final north metope of the Parthenon, the only one on this side not to have been removed by the Christians (cast). The seated figure on the right is usually identified as Hera, queen of the gods, whilst the standing one with the himation and peplos cloak most plausibly represents her daughter Hebe. Both are in an exceptional state of preservation, in contrast with the other figures of the north metopes of which only the outlines survive.

brimmed hat). Green pigment has been found in the folds of his chlamys. There where it is definitely worth lingering longer is at the middle block (*W VIII, 15*), where the horseman attempts to control his horse, propping up his right leg on a rock. This inventive composition, the realistic rendering of the animal's anatomy as well as of the folds of the rider's chlamys indicate the work of a leading artist, and experts attribute it to Phidias himself. As for the horseman, he is identified as either one of the two Athenian *hipparchs* (cavalry commander) or as the hero Theseus, the mythical founder of the Panathenaic festival. An interesting detail in the adjacent composition is the panther skin over the chiton of one of the two horsemen, a characteristic of the Thracian costume that had been adopted by the Athenian cavalry. Other horsemen follow, some on their horses, others next to them, heading for block *W II, 2-3*, where the first two riders pull hard on the bridals in order to stop them from running ahead. The phalanx leader turns towards the first horseman and, with raised hand, fixes his wreath on his hair.

North Side

The metopes

Despite the occasional doubts and questions that have arisen, scholars have concluded that the north metopes of the Parthenon represent scenes from the fall of Troy. Myth holds that the allied kings of Greece campaigned against the Asia Minor city after Helen, the divinely beautiful wife of king Menelaus of Sparta, was abducted by the Trojan prince Paris. The episodic siege of Troy, which nurtured the birth of one of the two Homeric epics, the *Iliad*, lasted for ten years and ended with the occupation of the city by the Greeks.

The narrative on the north metopes of the Parthenon begins in the northeast, where *Athena descends from her chariot*, while next to her *two Greek warriors disembark from a ship*. Further along *Philoctetes* and *Neoptolemus*, the son of Achilles, are preparing for battle, followed by a *horseman with a horse* and *two warriors*. Further along, at the other edge of the Gallery, are representations of *Aethra*, mother of Theseus, and her grandson *Demophon*, *Menelaus* and the cunning king of Ithaca *Odysseus* all searching for Helen, and *Helen* seeking sanctuary with the *xoanon* cult statue of Athena, with the goddess *Aphrodite* and the young *Eros* on her shoulder standing at the side. The other metopes

Block II, 3-6 from the north side of the Parthenon frieze. Three youths, wrapped in their himations with their heads slightly bowed and thoughtful, lead oxen to the place of sacrifice, one of which resists. The hand of a fourth man can be seen at the edge, attempting to discipline the beast. The high artistic standards of this piece place it amongst the finest of Attic art, and it is attributed to Phidias himself.

Part of the north frieze of the Parthenon. Block XI, 44 on the right has a marshal twisting his body back in an effort to stop the charge of the horses and to protect the elderly men who are walking ahead. Next to him we can see a section of the procession of these sixteen elders, who walk towards the east. Scholars believe that they were thallophoroi (elders holding olive branches) or city officials (athlothetes, competition judgers, or ieropoioi, overseers of religious rites).

Block XXIII, 63-65 of the north frieze featuring a marshal and a chariot with an apobates hoplite. The apobates contest was a chariot race during which the athletes (apobates), armed with helmet and shield, would jump from the moving chariot and then jump back onto it. Because the charioteers drove the chariot so as to help the apobates, the victory went to both of them. The presence of horses and chariots on the Parthenon frieze adds variety and makes the composition as a whole even more exciting.

feature: the king of Argos *Diomedes* with the *Palladion* of Troy (the sacred *xoanon* of the goddess Athena); the Trojan hero *Aeneas* helping his family to escape (one myth holds that Aeneas travelled to Sicily and Italy where his descendants later founded Rome); *Selene* on horseback travelling to the west; two unidentified and very ruinous gods; Zeus and Iris; and, finally, metope 32 with *Hebe* and *Hera*.

The frieze

On this side, the narration begins with a preparation scene: a horseman, still on foot, bends his head in an attempt to fix his clothing whilst a young servant with his master's himation thrown over his shoulder ties up his belt. Further ahead, another horseman has one hand on the reins of his frisky horse whilst with the other he fixes a band on his head. There follows a variety of stances, gaits and reactions of these proud creatures to the pull on their reins. Our attention is drawn to the image on block N XXXIV, 89-92: a marshal, with raised hand, gives an order to the approaching horsemen. In front of him, a well-built horseman with a chlamys wrapped in the hand that holds the reins turns to look back. After the procession of the horsemen, a representation of one of the most popular of the Panathenaic games, the *apobates* contest begins at block N XXVIII, 73-74. In this contest, the athletes, who were known as *apobates*, were hoplites who, whilst wearing their helmet and holding their shields had to jump down from a moving chariot, run, and then climb on again at the back of the chariot without it stopping. One of the figures represented, the *apobate* on block N XXI, 61-62 wears a long chiton tied crosswise with straps in order to facilitate his movements and has his shield on his back; scholars have identified this figure as Erechtheus, the mythical founder of the *apobates* contest. Also of interest is block N XII, 45-47, where the *apobate* is on the ground whilst the charioteer pulls with strength on the reins, a sign that the chariot has stopped. Beside it, a marshal in a himation looks back and gives the stop sign. Another marshal on block N XI, 44, attempts, by leaning back, to calm his galloping horses so as to protect the group of elders marching ahead. These sixteen male elders, who walk slowly towards the east or are standing conversing or turn to look back, have been interpreted as either *thallophoroi* (elders with olive branches) or as city officials (prize-awarding judges or overseers of sacred rites). After the elders there comes a procession of cithara and flute-players. This is followed by the exceptional block with the *hydrophorai*, youth who carried vases filled with water for sacrifices. Further ahead, on block N V, 13-15, are three *skaphephoroi*, youths who carried *skaphai* (trays) with offerings for the libation, on N IV, 9-12 three youths leading four rams to sacrifice, while on N III, 6-8 three youths lead two oxen. On block N II, 3-6, in a scene that adds a note of intensity to the smooth flow of the procession, one of the oxen jumps and resists the pull of the rope (it was painted on) by the driver, whose body continues on block N III. Almost nothing remains of this last block, which shows the driver of the first animal and a marshal, as we know from Carrey's sketches.

A fragment of the top right-hand corner of *block V* of the north frieze has been placed in a separate case, beneath the metopes. On it we can see the head of a young *skaphephoros* with part of his tray, which he held over his left shoulder.

South side

The metopes

The theme selected for the metopes of the south side was the mythical battle between *Lapiths*, a Thessalian people, and *Centaurs*, mythical creatures who had the form of a horse from the waist down. The king of the Lapiths was Perithous, a close friend and companion in various

The first two metopes (casts) on the south side of the Parthenon, adorned with scenes from the Centauromachy, the battle between Lapiths and Centaurs. Interpreting the central metopes on this side is of particular interest. Various theories have been expressed, such as that they represent the myth of Phaedra, second wife of the Athenian hero Theseus after the Amazon Antiope, or that of Alkestes, who sacrificed herself to save the life of her husband Admetos. Another view holds that the metopes represent individuals connected to the heroes of the Centauromachy and scenes from the wedding of king Perithous.

ventures to Theseus, the great hero of Athens. At Perithous' wedding to Deidameia, Perithous invited the Centaurs, who got drunk and attempted to grab the bride and the remaining Lapith women. The battle that followed became known as the *Centauromachy*. Of the 32 executed by Phidias' teams, the central *metopes 11* and *13-25* were destroyed in the disastrous explosion of 1687, although we can reconstruct them through their fragments with the help of Carrey's sketches. Moreover, some of these, *13-21*, have inspired much discussion as they appear to constitute a separate thematic unit that is difficult to interpret. In terms of technique scholars have distinguished the participation of many artists on the south metopes, some of whom were major sculptors such as Myron, Alcamenes and Phidias himself, whilst others were less able. A wonderful piece in terms of its composition and artistry is *metope 1*, with a Centaur grabbing a Lapith by the neck and preparing to hit him with the branch of a tree that today does not survive. His opponent, with a raised left leg, attempts to push him away and at the same time strike the horse's leg with his spear, which was perhaps a bronze addition. Of the other metopes, particularly fine are *metope 27* where the Centaur, turning his hand back, struggles to free himself from the spear that has been stuck in his side by a young Lapith (some scholars identify this figure with Theseus); *metope 28*, with the triumphant Centaur, leopard skin hanging from his left hand, trampling over the lifeless body of his rival; and, *metope 30* with the Centaur grabbing the half-kneeling Lapith by the hair. As for the two newly-weds, Perithous and Deidameia, some have identified them with the male figure in *metope 7* and the female figure in *metope 10*.

The frieze

This side has survived in the worst condition as a large part of it was destroyed in the 1687 explosion. Using the drawings of Carrey and Stuart, however, we can form an almost complete picture of what it was like. The representation begins, in correlation with the north side, with a procession of horsemen divided into ten groups (the prevalence of the number ten on the south frieze refers, according to some scholars, to the ten *phylai* or tribes into which Kleisthenes divided the Athenians for political and administrative purposes). At the start of the south frieze the visitor will see the *third block* on this side with the traces of Lord Elgin's team's attempts to remove its relief sculpture and, opposite, a copy of the relief. Of the ten groups of six horsemen, the best-preserved are blocks *S X26-28* and *S XI 29-31*, and it is worth observing the variety in the rendering of the manes of the galloping horses. After the horsemen come the carriages of the *apobates* contest, just as on the north side. Despite the fragmentary state of preservation the visitor will be able to distinguish some stunning flashes: on block *S XXXI, 78, 79*, for example, the *apobate* with the flowing chlamys turns back as the chariot rushes on, as we can see from the legs and the flowing manes of the horses. This is followed by a parade of eighteen elders; one interpretation believes that eight of them were Athenian archons (the ninth appears in the *peplos* presentation scene on the east frieze) and the others were the representa-

The impressive lion's head false sima *from the northeast corner of the Parthenon. The marble lion's heads in which the marble sima (gutter) of the temple ended were not perforated and were only decorative. Parthenon Gallery.*

View of the east side of the Parthenon Gallery with the pedimental sculptures on the first level. Unfortunately the protagonists of this scene, Zeus and Athena, have not survived, leading to many discussions amongst the experts as to their appearance. One view holds that Zeus was at the centre, seated on a throne, although in the past few decades most scholars have been of the opinion that the king of the gods was standing upright, flanked by Athena on one side, also standing upright, and his wife Hera on the other.

tives of the ten tribes. Further on, four figures (which do not survive) enigmatically hold rectangular objects, perhaps tablets with lists of accounts or *cithars*, followed by eight blocks with youths driving oxen to sacrifice. Block *S XLIII, 130-131* is impressive, with one driver attempting to return an ox into line, placing his foot on a rock so he can pull the rope with more strength.

East side

The pediment

The myth of the birth of Athena from Zeus' head appeared in a representation the central section of which was removed in the 6th cen-

The Parthenon was a temple dedicated to the goddess Athena, the patron of Athens, the east side of which appears to refer to all the gods of Olympus. The pediment shows the birth of Athena from Zeus' head in the presence of the other gods, whilst on the metopes the gods of Olympus fight the huge, ruthless Giants. The gods dominate the frieze with their presence, seated at the centre of the composition. In this way the Athenians may have wished to call upon the protection of all the gods that they worshipped, and not just Athena.

tury AD, when the Parthenon was being converted into a Christian church for the construction of the apse. The centre of the pediment was occupied by the two great gods, *Zeus* and *Athena*, whilst around them had been positioned figures that scholars have identified, with varying levels of success, as members of the ancient Greek pantheon. More specifically, on the left edge of the pediment, the brawny young man comfortably seated with his left leg bent is identified as the god of wine *Dionysus*. Behind him, seated on low caskets, are two female figures, one of which leans her arm on the shoulder of the other, in a tender gesture. Scholars conclude that these are the goddess of agriculture and vegetation *Demeter* and her dearly beloved daughter *Persephone*. They are followed by a young woman who has been identified as *Artemis* (*as well as with Hebe, Hecate and Eileithyia*), the *Peplos Figure Wegner* (named after the archaeologist M. Wegner) recognisable as *Hera*, the upper part of a man's body which is presumed to have belonged to *Hephaestus* (or *Ares*, or *Poseidon*), and three female figures with richly-pleated clothes, the first of which was *Hestia*, goddess of the house, or *Leto*, mother of *Apollo*, and next to her is *Dione*, mother of Aphrodite, or *Artemis*, followed by the goddess of beauty *Aphrodite*. At the two corners jump out *Helios* in his carriage rising on the left, and *Selene* setting on the right, framing the scene within the duration of a day. Of the horses of *Selene* the best-preserved is the second from the left, which is housed in the British Museum. The panting animal with the half-opened mouth and distended nostrils, which has been described as the perfect horse, is justifiably believed to be a work of the great sculptor Phidias.

To the left, in a separate space, the visitor can see four fragments attributed to this pediment: *section of a head* that belonged to *Helios* or *Hera* (Acr. 2381); the *left hand of Zeus with the lighting bolt* (Acr. 20.049); *lyre sound-box in the shape of a tortoise shell*, with the remnants of a hand (of Apollo, Acr. 6673); and, the *head of a goddess with a head-dress* attributed to *Eileithyia*, goddess of childbirth, or to *Selene* (Acr. 935). To the right is a *lion's head/false sima* (not perforated, simply decorative) from the northeast corner of the Parthenon.

The metopes

As the myth tells us, the time came when the gods of Olympus were forced to face the attack of the Giants, huge creatures which accord-

The horses of Selene's chariot, only the heads of which can be seen. The most eroded are the originals, whilst the finer and better preserved are casts, the originals of which are in the British Museum. Corresponding representations of Helios and Selene can be found on the east and north metopes of the Parthenon. As scholars have observed, personifications of heavenly bodies driving their chariots begin to appear in Attic vase-painting a little after the completion of the Parthenon, demonstrating the temple's influence on other art forms.

ing to one version had been born to Gaia in order to take revenge on the gods for the harsh punishment of her children, the Titans. This cosmogonic battle ended with the gods, of course, as victors.

Despite the bad state of preservation, scholars have been able to identify the figures thanks to Gigantomachy scenes on other monuments and, especially, red-figure vases. According to the experts, on *metope 1* a god, *Hermes*, strikes a giant, as happens also on *metope 2*, where the god under attack is *Dionysus* accompanied by a panther. A bronze snake was clearly wrapped around the leg of the giant, as can be seen from the outline and the drill holes. This is followed by battles between *Ares* and a giant, *Athena, Nike* and a giant, whilst next to them *Amphitrite* drives her chariot towards her husband Poseidon. Poseidon himself, on the neighbouring metope, is crushing a giant with Nisyros (an island whose volcanic activity was associated with the legend of the crushed giant attempting to escape). These are followed by *Hera* driving a chariot with winged horses, *Zeus* battling with a giant, *Apollo* kicking his opponent, *Artemis* driving the chariot of her brother Apollo, *Herakles* and *Eros* beating a giant (Herakles' contribution was decisive for the god's victory), *Aphrodite* chasing another and Hephaestus defeating his own opponent. The succession of the metopes comes to a close with *Helios* in his four-horse chariot rising from the sea. Scholars believe that Helios – the Sun – rose once the battle was concluded in the gods' favour.

The Frieze

The great climax of the Parthenon frieze. On block E I,1 a marshal, with raised right hand, looks back towards the animals arriving with their drivers, thus linking the procession on the south side with that on the east. Correspondingly, on the east side, on block E IX, a woman concludes the north procession of women. Further ahead, on both sides, there were groups of women. To the left, on block E II, 2-6 and on the next, E III, 7-19, sixteen young women, some with phiales (ritual vessels) in their hands move towards the centre of the frieze. In front of them are two male figures believed to be eponymous heroes, i.e. ancestral heads of two of the ten tribes of Attica. One of these, 18, may have represented Theseus. To the right, on blocks E VIII, 57-61 and E VII, 49-56 are more women, some of whom are holding phiales and one a censer, as well as two marshals. There follow four men to the left, leaning on staffs, and another four on the right who represent the rest of the eponymous heroes. At this point the style changes. Seated on stools, much larger in size than the other figures, are the gods of Olympus divided into two groups, apparently awaiting the arrival of the two sections of the processions. On the left *Hermes* appears first, with his *petasos*, the characteristic broad-brimmed hat, on his knees. His *kerykeion*, the herald's sceptre that was a symbol of the herald of the gods, would have been attached to the hole next to his right palm. His brother *Dionysus* leans familiarly on his shoulder. Behind, the seated female figure with the torch in her left hand is *Demeter*, whilst the male figure holding his bent knee in his two hands has been identified as the war god Ares. This group concludes with the divine royal couple of *Zeus* and *Hera*, he leaning comfortably on the back of his seat, a throne, and she looking towards him in the gesture of 'revealing' well-known from ancient vases (lifting the himation that covers her head by the edges). Next to Hera is a beautiful winged goddess, *Iris* or *Hebe*, gathering her hair in her left hand, which had loosened as she flew. On the other side, on the right, in front of the eponymous heroes, sits a very ruined *Aphrodite*, on whose knees her son *Eros* leans carefree, holding a sunshade (umbrella). Behind Aphrodite is *Artemis*, fixing her chiton with one hand whilst the other is tenderly passed around her sister's forearm, and Apollo turning round to talk with his uncle, the god of the sea Poseidon. They are followed by the goddess *Athena* and, by her side, *Hephaestus* with his staff beneath his arm, reminding us that he was a crippled god. Finally, in the centre of the two groups of gods, the much-discussed, enigmatic *scene of the presentation of the peplos* unfolds. Also enigmatic are the positions of the gods, who sit with their backs turned against the scene (perhaps, according to one view, the artist who designed the frieze wanted to indicate that they are invisible). To the left of the scene, two girls carry stools on their heads (one also holds something else, perhaps a small animal), and a woman in a chiton and himation, identified as the priestess of Athena, prepares to take the stool from the head of the first girl. A mature man in a long chiton next to her may, according to one version, have been the *archon basileus*, the king archon, who after the foundation of democracy had only religious duties. He receives the *peplos* from the hands of a little girl, whom some scholars believe to have been an Arrhephoros, one of the two little girls who wove the *peplos* in which the *diipetes* (heaven-sent) wooden cult statue of the goddess Athena would have been dressed. Others believe this figure to be a boy. With this scene, which has led to many, still unanswered questions, the creative, artistically brilliant representation of the Panathenaic procession on the Parthenon frieze comes to a close.

Level I: West Section

Returning to the lower floor, the visitor enters the section of the exhibition dedicated to the classical period and later.

The Propylaia

This section includes architectural pieces and sculptures from the *Propylaia*, the monumental entrance to the sanctuary of Athena on the Acropolis, as well as a model of the building. As we know from the descriptions of Pausanias, the celebrated 2nd-century AD traveller, the Propylaia of the Acropolis were adorned by works of famous artists, such as the Lemnian Athena by Phidias and the Hermes Propylaios by Alcamenes. The exhibits in this unit include two panels from the roof of the west hall of the central area, and a 1st-century BC head of *Hermes Propylaios*, a copy of an original work by Alcamenes *(Acr. 2281)*, as well as the *head of a herm* of the 2nd century AD *(Acr. 14877)*. Hermaic stelai, or Herms, were square stone pillars with the head of the god Hermes on top and male genitals carved on them about halfway up. They were set up at various points, such as crossroads in the town and countryside.

The Caryatids of the Erectheion. The slender girls, in a Π arrangement, supported the roof of the porch on their heads. Similar sculptures had been used on older buildings, for example the Treasury of the Siphnians at Delphi. The design of the figures, the excellent rendering of the pleats on their costumes and the artistic expression in general, make the porch of the Caryatids one of the most famous monuments in the world.

The Erechtheion

The next stop is the *Erechtheion*, the intricate sanctuary complex that the Athenians had dedicated to Athena Polias and Poseidon-Erechtheus. The first exhibits here, near a model of the Erechtheion, are one of the two *building inscriptions* that were built into the wall with information on its construction, as well as the Ionic *frieze* and the north porch. The frieze does not appear to have a homogenous subject. Specialists have identified gods, heroes and mortals in the figures that adorn it, scenes related to the cults that were housed in the Erechtheion. The artist who designed it remains unknown although, by contrast, the building inscriptions that have survived reveal to us the names of some of the sculptors who worked on it as well as other

The back view of the Caryatids. In this Museum, for the first time, visitors have the opportunity to admire the sculptures of the ancient Acropolis in the round. Here, one can observe the ornate hairstyles of these Athenian korai; each is slightly different and they are believed to have been created by different artists.

Detail of one of the Caryatids. Her long hair, loosely tied, falls down her back, whilst at the front it gracefully frames her youthful face. An architectural piece, similar to a basket-shaped column capital with 'egg' decoration, sat between the heads of the korai and the roof of the porch.

interesting information, such as their fees: 60 drachmas on average for one figure, 120 drachmas for two. Further along, in an area designed like a balcony, so as to be reminiscent of the south porch of the Erechtheion, the famous Caryatids proudly stand (five of them, since the sixth is in the British Museum). Dressed in a belted Doric *peplos* and short himation, with their hair in complex plaits, sandals on their feet and snake bracelets, these marble korai stood in for the columns on this section of the building. Their hands have been lost, although it is believed on the basis of Roman copies found in Italy that in their right hands they held phiales (shallow vessels for drinking and libations), whilst with their left hands they raised the edge of their garments. Scholars believe that they were made by different artists, perhaps from the workshop of the celebrated sculptor Alcamenes, a student and collaborator of Phidias. There are also various interpretations of the Caryatids, the most convincing being that they were *choephoroi* (libation bearers). The south porch was located over the tomb of the mythical Athenian king Kekrops; in other words, it was his earthly monument and the Caryatids perhaps represented the women who performed *choai* in honour of the glorious dead (*choai* were a type of offering to the dead, whereby a liquid was poured into the earth over their grave from a special vessel). Returning to the central area and proceeding towards the right, the visitor will be able to admire a bronze *lamp in the shape of a warship*, which bears the inscription 'sanctuary of Athena' and was found inside the Erechtheion (*NAM X 7038*, late 5th c. BC). Further behind stands the second building inscription.

Temple of Athena Nike

The section on the *temple of Athena Nike* follows, the small Ionic temple constructed within a tall rectangular tower to the right as one ascends the stairs leading to the Propylaia. Particularly impressive are the panels from the *parapet*, a type of guardrail that protected the three sides of the tower. Their external surfaces are adorned with relief scenes, featuring winged Nikes and the honoured goddess Athena. This was a work by a team of artists led by Phidias' other renowned student Agoracritus and dating to 421-413 BC or, according to another theory, the last decade of the 5th century BC. It is considered the most important manifestation of the 'rich style', the prevailing art style of the last two decades of the 5th century BC, which in sculpture is characterised by the rich folds of dress, original poses and affected movements, and thematic and figurative innovations. The panels are arranged in a Π-shape, enabling the visitor to admire *Nikes*

Winged Nike, leaning on her left leg, raising her right foot and bending over to tie up her sandal. The rendering of the costume, with its rich pleats beneath which her body can be seen, is impressive. Panel from the marble parapet of the temple of Athena Nike, one of the finest examples of the skill and imagination of the late-5th century BC artists. Level I, West section, Acr. 973.

leading a bull to sacrifice and others decorating a *trophy with weapons.* On one panel we see the goddess *Athena seated on a rock* with her shield leaning by her side. On another a *Nike climbing up some stairs.* There is also the masterpiece *Nike adjusting her sandal*: Nike, in a thin see-through chiton that slips and reveals her shoulder, bends to adjust the sandal on her raised right foot. Another piece from the workshop of Agoracritus and exceptional example of the 'rich style' is the *frieze* of the temple of Athena Nike a little further down. On the east side are representations of an Agora (conference) of the Olympian gods (some believe the subject is the birth of Athena), whilst in the other three panels intense battle scenes unfold. It has been argued that these are mythological battles although the prevailing view holds that these were historical battles: Marathon (490 BC), Plataea (479 BC), Athens against Megara (458 BC). This section ends with a model of the temple of Athena Nike.

The cases

The wall cases at the back of the Gallery contain many exhibits, some connected to the buildings described above. Case 28 contains *votives in the severe style*, such as *statuette heads* including the *head of an athlete* (*13*, 480-470 BC) and a *youth on a dolphin*, part of a vase decoration (*9*, 474-450 BC). Case 29 includes fragments of beautiful *red-figure vases* and a *white-ground vase*, with the signatures of their painters, whilst pieces of a *black-figure amphora* of 550-540 BC have been placed in case 30. Also black-figure are the vases in case 31, with a representation of *two wrestlers and a spectator* (*3*, 500-450 BC), followed in case 32 by *lamps* of various types, dating from 600 BC to the 1st century BC, and in case 33 *terracotta statuettes* such as a *child seated with his toy bag on his knees* (*2*, 350-300 BC), a *child's head* (*15*, 350-300 BC) and a beautiful *head of Athena* (*23*). Case 34 exhibits *fragments of sculptures from the pediments of the temple of Athena Nike*, with scholars believing that the east pediment perhaps featured a Gigantomachy, while case 35 contains *fragments from the parapet of the temple of Athena Nike*. This is followed by seven open cases, without glass, where one can see other *sculptures from the parapet of the temple of Athena Nike*.

Level I: North section, 5th century BC – 5th century AD

The north section of the Gallery Π focuses on the *votives* set up on the Acropolis from the 5th century BC onwards as well as *stelai* with *decrees* passed by the *Boule* (council) or the *deme* of Athens, which were also set up on the Acropolis from the mid-5th century BC. The decrees are divided into two categories: treaties and Athens' alliances with other cities, and honorary decrees passed in honour of personages who offered services or benefaction to the city. The original texts, before their official publication, were written on papyrus or wooden tablets.

Sections of a votive relief, known as the *Lenormant relief* (Acr. *1339*), with a rare representation of a trireme (warship with three series of oars), introduce us to this section of the Gallery. This was the 'Paralos', one of the Athenian state sacred ships used on various sacred or public missions. In the representation, in addition to the hunched oarsmen and the captain we see, above right, the hero Paralos, the inventor, according to the myth, of sailing (late 5th century BC). The adjacent exhibits are *two votive relief bases*, one with the

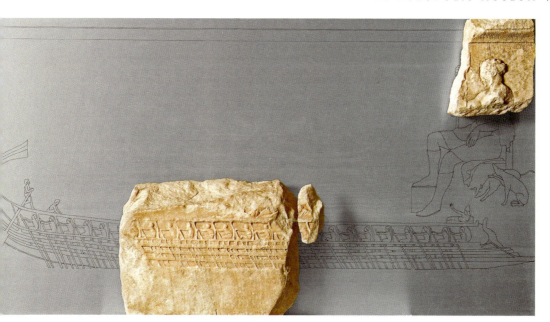

Section of a votive relief (Lenormant) with the representation of a trireme. The original composition showed the Athenian ship manned with twenty-five rowers. The larger-than-life, in relation to the ship, youthful figure above right is identified as the hero Paralos. Level I, North section, Acr. 1339.

The representation of a trireme on the Lenormant relief is a reminder that in the classical period Athens grew powerful and dominant in the east Mediterranean thanks to its military fleet. The effective functioning of the fleet required the labour of a large number of rowers, who came from the fourth and lowest income group of ancient Athens, the thetes.

Section of an inscribed decree stele in honour of the Samians. At the end of the Peloponnesian War, when the Spartans crushed the Athenian fleet at Aegospotami, almost all the Athenians' allies abandoned them out of fear or choice. Only the Samians stayed by their side and for this reason the Athenian demos, in gratitude, chose to honour them. The stele in the illustration includes a copy of this decree from 405 BC, and below two complementary decrees from 403-2 BC. On the upper part of this relief Hera, patron of Samos, and Athena, patron of Athens, clasp hands in friendship. Level I, North section, Acr. 1333.

representation of an *apobates contest* (a man in full armour would jump from and climb back onto a moving chariot, *Acr. 1326*, late 4th or early 3rd century BC) and the other with the *bronze votive of a choregos sponsor of the dramatic contests* (*Acr. 1338*, 329 or 323 BC), with youths wearing himations at a musical contest and others, nude, with their shields dancing the martial Pyrrhic dance. Further behind, towards the centre of the Gallery, stands the famous group of *Procne and Itys* (*Acr. 1358*, 430 BC), a votive and perhaps a work of the sculptor Alcamenes (myth holds that Procne, daughter of the mythical king of Athens Pandion, killed her son Itys in order to take revenge on her husband Tereus for raping and torturing her sister Philomela). Another

This colossal female head, found near the southeast corner of the Propylaia in the 19th century, has been identified as the head of the cult statue of Artemis Brauronia. According to the 2nd-century AD traveller Pausanias the statue that adorned the goddess's sanctuary on the Acropolis was created by the famed 4th-century BC sculptor Praxiteles. The facial features were perhaps deliberately destroyed when Christianity became the dominant religion in Athens. 330 BC. Level I, North section, Acr. 1352

work by a famous artist, Praxiteles, is the colossal *head* of the cult statue of *Artemis Brauronia*, the patron goddess of labour and pregnant women (*Acr. 1352*, 330 BC). Adjacent, it is worth observing the charming small *bear*, an animal sacred to Artemis, goddess of hunting (*Acr. 3737*, 4th century BC). Various exhibits have been placed around, primarily a group of *decrees*, decorated on the upper part with reliefs of figures associated with the content, amongst them: Athena and Hera, patron goddesses of the two cities clasping hands on the *honorary decree of the Samians* (*Acr. 1333*, 405/4 and 403/2 BC); the *deme* of Athens conversing with a female figure, a personification of Corcyra on the *alliance between the Athenians and the Corcyrans* (*NAM 1467*,

Bust of a barbarian leader, with idealised features. The figure with the thick tussled hair, finely-shaped lips, and soft facial features has been identified with various historical figures, such as the Bosporan kings Rhoemetalces and Sauromates II, as well as the Athenian benefactor Herodes Atticus. These identifications remain unconfirmed, however. 2nd century AD. Level I, North section, NAM 419.

376/5 BC); the goddess Athena seated on a throne with an eagle on her knees and a male figure in front on the *decree in honour of the consuls of Abydos*, a city in Asia Minor (*Acr. 1330*, first quarter 4th century BC); the god Ares between the honoured personage and a goddess on an *honorary decree after a military victory* (*NAM 2947*, third quarter 4th century BC). Further along, in a privileged position, the eye is drawn to a famous youthful *head of Alexander the Great*, either by the sculptor Leochares or a copy of a work by Lysippus, the only artist that the legendary leader trusted to create his sculptures (*Acr. 1331*, 336 BC). The area to the left of Alexander's bust is occupied by *decrees* and two impressive *votive bases*, one with *reliefs of athletes* (*Acr. 3176+*, 330 BC) and the other with *dancing female figures* (*Acr. 3363+*, early 4th century BC), whilst various exhibits are on the right, mainly *sculptures*. The standouts are an impressive *head of a female acrolithic statue* (a wooden sculpture with stone marble extremities and head) with eyes of inserted material, indicating a chryselephantine statue of the 5th or 4th century BC (*NAM 244*, 2nd century AD), as well as the *heads of the Athenian general Miltiades and the goddess Athena*, from a votive group, *Acr. 2344, 2338*, 2nd century AD). These last are considered copies of a group with many figures dedicated by the Athenians in 470-460 BC at the sanctuary of Apollo at Delphi, in commemoration of their victory against the Persians at Marathon (490 BC). There follows a series of sculptures of Athena, of various periods. Proceeding towards the end of the Gallery, the visitor encounters *Roman busts* including the *bust of a priest* (*NAM 356*, mid-2nd century AD) and the expressive *bust of a barbarian leader* (*NAM 419*, third quarter 2nd century AD). There follows another model of the Acropolis during this period, an imposing *marble throne of the* 2nd century AD with relief decoration (*Acr. 1366*), which was used as the bishop's throne in the Parthenon in the 5th century AD when it had been converted into a Christian church, an impressive *marble sphere with magical symbols* (*NAM 2260*, 2nd-3rd century AD), indicating the mystery practices of later antiquity and, finally, a *treasure* of the 7th century AD. This treasure, which was discovered in the Asclepeion in 1876, is comprised of *234 gold coins*, of which 177 date to the time of the emperor Constantine II (AD 641-668), and their excellent state of conservation indicates that they had not been put into circulation. The tour of the Gallery, and of the Museum, ends with the *portrait of a Neoplatonist philosopher*, of the 5th century AD (*Acr. 1313*), and a model of the medieval Acropolis.